MW01138658

How to Write a PhD in Less Than 3 Years

A practical guide

Steven Harrison

authorHOUSE®

AuthorHouse™ UK Ltd.
500 Avebury Boulevard
Central Milton Keynes, MK9 2BE
www.authorhouse.co.uk
Phone: 08001974150

First published by AuthorHouse 10/7/2010

ISBN: 978-1-4520-8995-9 (sc)

This book is dedicated to all those who recognise the importance of being grateful

'Les malheureux sont ingrats; cela fait partie de leur malheur'
Victor Hugo

Contents

A FEW WORDS ABOUT THE AUTHOR

Steven Harrison is a pen name for a recognised legal practitioner. The author of several academic publications, Steven wrote his PhD thesis while working full-time for a leading financial institution, submitting it for examination within 24 months of becoming registered as a research student in one of the UK's top Law Schools. His doctoral thesis has since been published as a monograph by a leading international publisher and is the main reference work in its field.

FOREWORD

While PhD-writing is, no doubt, a highly demanding task, it is far from 'mission impossible'. Large numbers of women and men have taken on this task successfully and, no doubt, thousands more will follow. The purpose of this short book (which *has* to be short if it is to serve its purpose) is to provide some practical advice and guidance on the issues involved in conceptualising, organising and writing your doctoral thesis, so that you can increase your chances of surviving the intellectual and psychological ordeal of PhD thesis writing with the least amount of pain and with the minimum investment in terms of the time spent pursuing your objective.

Having seen others fail, some of them undeservedly, and others yet suffer, many of them unnecessarily, I set out to share with you my successful PhD thesis writing experience, hoping to be able to help you decide whether or not you want to start a PhD in the first place and, if yes, how you may want to go about it as well as what you will need to do in order to complete it without unnecessary delay.

This short book is divided into an Introduction, followed by four Parts. The Introduction has something to say about the author of this book, its subject matter as well as you, its reader, whatever your interest in it, academic or otherwise. Part One addresses the more conceptual considerations of relevance to PhD-writing, such as a candidate's choice of research topic, its translation into a thesis proposal, the achievement of the originality and substantial contribution requirements and a candidate's choice of methodology. Parts Two and Three address the more practical aspects of the doctoral degree process, including registration and writing, with an emphasis on the choice of supervisor and school, some of the nitty-gritty of academic writing, the candidate's organisation and the management of her time, the sequence of writing and pitfalls to be avoided at all costs. Part Four addresses issues of relevance to your *viva* and its aftermath. It is followed by a Postlude, summarising the author's main recommendations to research degree (or aspiring research degree) candidates.

It is my sincere hope that you will find reading this book fruitful and that you will consider the account of my doctoral thesis writing experiences contained in its pages to be thought-provoking and, most of all, useful.

Steven Harrison, August 2010

INTRODUCTION

1. Why is the author qualified to write this book?

Personal experience and a genuine desire to share it are the author's main assets and aspirations, respectively. He has been through the PhD thesis-writing process successfully and feels he has some useful tips to share through the pages of this short book on how the challenge of writing a doctoral thesis can best be handled. At the same time, not being a professional academic 'with an axe to grind', the author has good reasons to believe that his take on the issues addressed in this book will be more easily accessible to the average reader and his views less tainted with the professional bias underlying some of the extant works on this topic.

These are his credentials: the author completed his PhD thesis in 27 months, inclusive of the three-month waiting period between the submission of his thesis and its defence. Although he did have a modest capital of writing experience that he could build on, this was his first major piece of writing ever. Moreover, the author wrote his PhD while working full-time (from a responsible and commitment-intensive position), without 'recycling' for the purposes of his thesis any of his professional work. During this 27 month period the author lived a, more or less, normal life: he travelled (including for the purposes of his PhD), he published (*inter alia* on non PhD-related topics), he went on holidays and he kept in touch with friends and family. And yet, he managed to complete his PhD research and writing in slightly over two years. 'Is he, perhaps, an exceptionally gifted and extraordinarily talented person, whose experience can only be of limited relevance to the average candidate?' I hear you ask. As much as the author would have liked that to have been the case, the answer is 'no'. 'Did he have a very strong academic predisposition or inclination towards research?' some of you may ask. Again the answer is 'no', even if some further qualifications are, this time, apposite: the author was, certainly, an above average undergraduate student (even if by no means an outstanding one), having held a '2:1' degree from one of the better Law Schools in the UK and a postgraduate degree awarded with 'Merit' from another (slightly better) Law School, also in the UK, before he took up a research degree in London; moreover, he had already had some experience with publishing prior to taking up his PhD degree (having, therefore, had a modest capital of writing experience that he could draw on for the purposes of his research work). However, never was the author awarded any academic distinctions or prizes (and not because he never entered a competition) nor did he otherwise leave his mark as an extraordinary student. 'Did the author have any other links to the academic community that helped him take up and finish his PhD sooner rather than later?' Certainly not: the author had never set eyes on his supervisor before their first meeting and was, at the time of his application for admission as a research student, something of an 'unknown quantity', having for several years been out of academia (including for a two year stint of relative intellectual stagnation during his military service). 'Did the author perhaps 'recycle' work he had previously done in a different, non-academic capacity?' Not at all: his was original work, from beginning to end, conducted *after* he became registered as a postgraduate research student. 'Did he enjoy the benefit of decisive external assistance with his work, helping him finish sooner than one would normally expect?' Again, the answer is 'no', although he would often discuss his research work with colleagues, friends and family to sound their (mostly) non-expert take on some of his ideas and to test their robustness. What the author did, however, do was to follow the advice dispensed in the pages of this short book (and which he mostly had common sense to thank for) and to prosecute, with quasi-religious devotion, the routine explained below. Curious? Just read through and you will know enough to be able to visualise yourself doing just as well (or, why not, better), learning from the most reliable source of information there is: somebody else's personal experience.

One word of caution is apposite for the benefit of the reader. Writing a PhD thesis involves, somewhat unsurprisingly, a good deal of (formal) writing. This is a skill that cannot be acquired through reading up on other people's reflections on the subject of 'writing': it is a skill the acquisition of which involves effort and, most of all, daily, persistent practice. The purpose of this book – which is addressed mainly to UK University doctoral degree candidates (or prospective candidates) from the fields of humanities and social sciences but which will, in many respects, be of relevance to candidates from other disciplines or studying in different parts of the world as well as to Master degree candidates whose work involves the writing of a dissertation –[1] is to 'demystify' the main aspects of the doctoral thesis writing exercise, to guide you through the key stages of your postgraduate research work and, most of all, to help you reach your objective sooner rather than later. The difficult tasks of choosing a promising research topic and of achieving an adequate level of scholarship in its examination remain yours throughout. Good luck!

2. Are you qualified to write a PhD?

This is a question that you are likely to have asked yourself several times prior to deciding to take-up postgraduate research studies (or that you may still be reflecting on if you have yet to become registered as a postgraduate research student). Answering that question presents, not unsurprisingly, an almost insuperable practical difficulty for anyone who has not been through the doctoral thesis writing process before (understandably, very few people will ever seek to go through this process more than once in their lifetime). It is only natural, therefore, that, this being an *academic* endeavour, candidates would feel the urge to draw on their academic experience, whether as undergraduates or as Masters' degree students, in order to gauge the likelihood of their success in this new and challenging endeavour, drawing comfort (or discomfort, as the case may be) from their record. A word of caution is apposite here, as some of the conclusions you may arrive at on the basis of your academic record are likely to be erroneous, unduly encouraging you or, instead, putting you off the idea of taking-up postgraduate research studies.

The truth is that your hitherto academic record can provide no safe or conclusive indications as to your future performance as a postgraduate research student. While this author is not aware that anything akin to a 'negative correlation' between the two might exist, it would be wrong to automatically deduce from one's brilliant (or not so brilliant, as the case may be) performance as an undergraduate student that one will either most certainly prosper or, conversely, flounder in one's PhD ambitions. This is because both the skills required for success in a taught course and the standards against which you will have been judged as an undergraduate student are, in several respects, different from those applicable in the case of postgraduate research degrees. Hard work, carefully targeted, 'selective' learning – geared towards maximising one's chances of success in one's end-year written examinations – and a certain amount of luck (in terms of an examinee's choice of examination questions) can take you a (very) long way as an undergraduate student, enabling you, to some extent, to 'work the system' and take advantage of its loopholes to enhance your performance.[2] The same is not true of PhD-writing, where hard work is no doubt necessary but where neither selective learning nor luck will be of any relevance to your success (unlike, for instance, the ability to work independently or to think critically, which can make all the difference between a successful and an unsuccessful candidate), and where your examiners (and, to some extent, your supervisors) are likelier to antagonize you than they are to treat you with the measure of leniency that they may have applied to you when you were an undergraduate student.[3]

If well-performing undergraduate students would be well advised not to take for granted that they will also do brilliantly in their postgraduate studies, the same is true of average undergraduate students who should not mechanistically or uncritically assume that because they have not done particularly well in the past, they are unlikely to have what it takes to succeed in their (perforce, more demanding) PhD studies (however counter-intuitive this may sound). If you should happen to fall in the latter group, ask yourself *why* it was that you were unable to distinguish yourself as an undergraduate student. If the reason is that you were too lazy to invest the time and effort required to do better or because your intellectual potential was (and, possibly, remains) somewhat limited, you would be right to deduce that you are likelier to encounter severe difficulties in your PhD-writing endeavours than you are to prosper in them. But if the reason for your mediocre record had anything to do with your objections, from a moral or substantive point of view, to selective learning, with your exceptionally bad luck on more than one occasions or with your poor examination technique, you would be wrong to presume that your past performance can determine your chances of doing well as a postgraduate research student.

In a nutshell, the author's advice to you is as follows. Provided that (i) you were, at least, an average undergraduate student, (ii) you have not 'burned yourself out' while studying for your undergraduate (or postgraduate, Masters') degree and (iii) you have shown signs of excellence in any enterprise you have embarked upon during or since the conclusion of your studies, you should avoid making any arbitrary associations between your academic record and your future performance or give up, too quickly, on your postgraduate research ambitions, fearing that you will, once again, under-perform. In the same vein, if your past performance had less to do with your individual intellectual potential than it had to do with your examination skills or other, exogenous factors, you would be well advised to temper your ambitions and approach the prospect of taking up a doctoral degree with more prudence and circumspection than your record would ostensibly justify, avoiding to fall into the 'complacency trap' that your past academic achievements are likely to lay for you.

3. Reasons for wanting to write a PhD

'Why may one want to write a PhD in the first place?' I can imagine some of you wonder (let alone in less than 3 years). The truth is that, unless your plan is to become a full-time academic, in which case a PhD will probably be an indispensable formal qualification for your appointment,[4] you are not likely to ever need a PhD. Moreover, depending on your professional orientation or actual line of business, a PhD may not add much to your *curriculum vitae* and could even be deemed to be an impediment, at least in some respects (suggesting, for instance, to some prospective employers that you are too much of a theoretically oriented and not practically-minded enough fellow).[5] However, there *are* a few reasons why you may still want to write a PhD even without any *professional* academic pretensions. The 'bad news' is that only some of these reasons will be the 'right' ones.

One reason why you may want to undertake postgraduate research even if you do not intend to work in academia is as a gift to yourself: the profound sense of satisfaction you will feel once you have achieved your objective is one that no amount of money can buy. From plain Mr or Ms Smith you will acquire a title that you will have deserved through your hard work and intellectual labour, as opposed to having inherited, however unmeritoriously or coincidentally, through your blood line and by right of birth. What is more, apart from representing an undisputable badge of competence that you can genuinely be proud of, for what it is worth, this is a title that you will carry along for ever, not a transitory gain. Field Marshals loose their privileges once they have retired and world champions their place in the podium after a few years in the limelight, however illustrious their careers or impressive the collection of their trophies. But not you! Your title, signalling your official entrance to the community of scholars, is yours for ever, as is the prestige (however modest) that goes along with it. Let us face it: it is not very frequently that one is 'upgraded' in so essential a way or that one's capabilities are so emphatically certified. Besides, a PhD can also be useful as a *professional* (as opposed to a purely academic) qualification, as the knowledge that you will hopefully have acquired through your research is likely to stand you in good stead in your professional environment, especially if there are synergies between the subject of your research and the nature of your employment.[6] Finally, your systematic exposure to formal writing for the duration of your research and the self-imposed discipline required for the research and writing stages of your work will inevitably improve your reasoning and drafting skills,[7] providing a first class opportunity for you to test and improve on your planning, time-management and, ultimately, independent leadership skills (even if you will not come out of your PhD experience a fundamentally different person, as most outsiders might think). To the extent that people are 'the sum of their experiences', your PhD-writing experience will, forever, represent a benchmark against which to measure the relative complexity of whatever other tasks you may be called upon to undertake later in life, helping you put these into perspective and overcome the practical and, most of all, the psychological hurdles that their accomplishment might entail.[8]

At the end of the day the best reason why you may want to write a PhD although you are not planning to take up a career in academia is a very simple and personal one: it is because you consciously want to (as opposed to having drifted into it, for whatever reason) *and* feel you can do it.[9] You do not need to have a strong academic background to feel the urge (although it no doubt helps, however subconsciously), nor is it essential that you plan devoting your entire life to research before you make up your mind that this is something you would genuinely want to devote some of your time and resources to. It is sufficient for you to decide that you want to engage in postgraduate research that you feel strong enough and sustained enough a desire to investigate a phenomenon, to examine an issue, to find answers to one or more questions, to test a hypothesis and that you are, of course, prepared to do this within the context of an organized academic process leading up to the award of a postgraduate research degree. In fact, it is only if you genuinely feel that urge and if you are prepared to take responsibility for your project that this author would advise you to start a PhD in the first place. You are otherwise unlikely to be successful and, even if you are, it will not be without a good deal of compulsive effort, exerting pressure on yourself to do something you do not have a genuine appetite for and which, somehow, is 'not you'. Remember this: motivation and tenacity are all-important ingredients for your success in this enterprise and these can only come from within. You cannot seriously consider embarking on as demanding an endeavour as a postgraduate research degree simply because you have seen others doing so or because you have only just finished your Masters' degree and would rather continue studying as opposed to taking up a 'real' job in the 'real' world, the reason being that superficial reasons such as these are unlikely to stand the test of time or see you through the trials and tribulations of postgraduate research.

Ask yourself if you really want to go through this and it is only if you can answer that question with an unambiguous 'yes' that you can feel reassured that you will not be starting something where you will be out of your depth, that will administer more pain than satisfaction and that will most certainly last (well) over 3 years, with all the implications of an extension in the duration of your studies for your finances, your well-being and sanity.

4. Reasons for wanting to write a PhD in less than 3 years

Having seen why you may want to write a PhD let us see why you may want to do it faster than in the 3, 4 or more years that most candidates take to complete their research degrees.

'Surely, a PhD should not be a race against the clock. It is a different sort of exercise, a noble, non syllabus-bound endeavour that differs fundamentally from other types of tertiary studies and which requires more time than they do' some of you may argue. That doctoral studies differ, both quantitatively and qualitatively, from other tertiary studies is, no doubt, true. But if doctoral studies can be accomplished to the requisite level of scholarship in a shorter time-span can there be any valid reasons to waste precious months or years writing one's PhD that one could use more profitably pursuing other, no less noble and possibly more gratifying projects? Apart from this general, *carpe diem*-resonant philosophical observation on the importance of acting on the opportunity of time and on the significance of putting it to the most advantageous use possible, there are other, more concrete and no less legitimate reasons why one may want to finish one's PhD sooner rather than later. Let us go over some of them (acknowledging, from the outset, that the following account is by no means an exhaustive one).

One obvious reason for wanting to prosecute your PhD as expeditiously as possible is that you may have something 'better', no less urgent or, perhaps, more important to do with your life (for instance, get married, have children, start a business or keep the elderly members of your family company in their old age). These considerations will apply more to those who have started their PhDs later in life (although younger candidates have every reason to avoid extending the time taken for the completion of their work, even if this is something that they cannot always appreciate early in their lives). Another consideration, of relevance to more mature students, may be this: if you are over 30 (or older), with a hard-earned station in life, you are likely to feel uncomfortable around fellow research students in their mid twenties or to resent being viewed as a 'student' by your supervisor or as a 'candidate' by your University (although this is exactly what you are).[10] Alternatively, you may want to limit the costs incurred in studying (including travelling and accommodation expenses, tuition fees etc.); as you will no doubt be aware, especially if you are an overseas student, education does not come cheap (at least not at this level), with the costs of studying having soared in recent years. Yet another reason why you may want to finish sooner rather than later is because you may have taken time off your work or continue in full-time employment while pursuing your studies (for instance, in order to be in a position to finance your PhD): in either of these cases you are likely to want the keep the disruption that writing your thesis entails as short as possible so as to be able to devote your undivided attention to your professional endeavours and avoid falling into disfavour (understandably so) with your employer (who is indirectly financing your postgraduate studies).[11] Another, more 'academic' but no less valid reason for wanting to make quick progress with your work is this: you may have good reasons to believe that there will sooner or later be developments in your field of research that you will want to anticipate. Especially if your topic is of current interest (a so-called 'moving target'), you are well advised to proceed with your work as rapidly as possible so that you can doubly capitalize on your intellectual toil by being the first to publish on your subject, averting the risk of some of your facts or conclusions having become outdated by the time your research work is finished.[12] After all, you cannot altogether exclude the (not so remote)[13] possibility that someone else may be writing on, more or less, the same topic as you are and be developing ideas very similar to yours: if they successfully complete their work and go public with their conclusions before *you* do, that will inevitably take some of the wind off your sails. It would certainly be a source of disappointment for you to be 'beaten to the punch' by someone else, even if only by a matter of weeks or months, despite all your hard work.[14]

A host of other, more or less 'practical' considerations are likely to have a bearing on your decision to press on with your research and writing instead of 'taking it easy'. For instance, you may want to use your PhD as an employment qualification, whether to take up an academic appointment or in order to achieve promotion within your service: stretching your studies over too long a period of time may mean missing out on 'once in a lifetime' opportunities and this is something that you can ill-afford to see happening, and certainly not in today's highly competitive world. Or you may just be the sort of person who performs better in shorter time spans and who cannot see sustained efforts through without losing your focus, in which case moving fast may make all the difference between proving successful or failing miserably, despite a promising start.

It follows that there can be very many legitimate reasons why you may want to complete your research degree as soon as possible (more than one of which may apply to one and the same candidate). At the end of the day, the most important reason for deciding to press on with your research work is this: however enjoyable, writing a doctoral thesis is a challenging (and, at times, almost frustrating) task that involves angst and stress over a sustained period of time, with even the most self-confident candidates coming to question, at one point in time or other, their commitment to soldiering on to the (not-so-) bitter end. If you cannot cope with stress over too long a period of time (nobody does, even if some can handle it better than others and despite the instrumentality of stress in helping the less motivated amongst us achieve their goals), you are better off finishing your work sooner rather than later. Just *what* it takes for that to be possible will be the subject matter of the following pages of this book.

PART I
CONCEPTUAL CONSIDERATIONS
THE PLANNING STAGE

5. Choice of research topic

Unless your doctoral studies are funded by a project grant, in which case your research topic is likely to be pre-determined, you will need to take time to reflect on your choice of research topic before you begin to entertain postgraduate research ambitions or, *a fortiori*, before you seriously embark upon research work. Choosing your research topic is something that you will need to do very, very carefully and with an open and critical mind as the outcome of your reflections is bound to have an impact on the successful and prompt completion of your studies.[15] There is no 'formula', as such, to help you decide what your research topic should be: this is a deeply personal choice that you will ultimately need to make yourself if you are to pursue it with the determination necessary to see your research through to its successful conclusion.[16] Some general principles do, nevertheless, apply, to help you organize your thinking and test its robustness before you seriously entertain the idea of starting a PhD in the first place (and, *a fortiori*, before you engage in any concrete writing). Here they are, not necessarily in descending order of importance.

A *first* rule of thumb is to avoid abstract research topics. Abstract, highly theoretical research topics are, in principle, to be avoided on account of their inherent vagueness and of the higher intellectual and cognitive demands that they place upon candidates compared to less ambitious, more straightforward topics. It is possible that you are someone very gifted, who can handle non-figurative thinking and formulate thoughts that logically cohere, notwithstanding their complexity and limited association to the 'real' world. Most of us, however, including the author of this book, do not fall in this category. Unless you are one of the 'lucky few' who can successfully navigate through the maze of abstract thinking, choosing a theoretical research topic - one which is not very firmly anchored to the 'real' world - can cast you in a difficult predicament, extending indefinitely the period of your research while you are trying to pin down your subject and to decide exactly what you want the focus of your research work to be.[17] Candidates (especially younger ones) have a predilection for abstract research subjects and something of a natural tendency for setting lofty and, perhaps, unrealistic research goals, whether because they labour under a (noble) misapprehension as to the impact of their work (remember, unless published, few PhDs are ever read after their successful completion by anyone other than those interested in the specific topic) or because they are not yet conscious of their limitations or because their exposure to the 'real' world is less extensive compared to their familiarity with the world of ideas to which they were exposed as students. Your enthusiasm for an exciting-sounding but abstract research topic should be tempered by the consideation that, at the end of the day, your main (even if *not* unique) objective is to fulfil an academic requirement. If this objective can be achieved through a choice of topic that you genuinely feel you can handle (however less exciting it might sound compared to a competing alternative, which, while more interesting, is harder to conceptualize) it would not be a wise decision for you to deliberately make your life (even more) difficult by consciously opting for the less manageable alternative.

A directly related point for the reader to take note of is the following. Some candidates wrongly assume that setting out with no more than a rough idea of where they want to get at with their research may not be such a bad idea since their reflections can be expected to mature as they progress with their research work. Again, it is possible that you are particularly gifted (or very lucky) and that clarity will, indeed, come to you before too long and, preferably, when you still have the forces to spare for concluding your work.[18] The likelihood is, however, small that you will fall within this select pool of the 'chosen' or the lucky few. It is only if, already from the outset, you have a more or less clear idea of what you want to write about – not just what your general research area is but, also, what your actual topic is to be – *and* how you want to develop that topic (both elements are equally important) that you can hope to be able to complete your research degree successfully (and, hopefully, also quickly) even if your final conclusion remains (as it should, at this early stage) open.[19] Otherwise, there is a risk that you may never finish your work (let alone in less than 3 years) and this is a risk that you are advised not to take, for obvious reasons.[20]

A *second* rule of thumb is to choose a topic from an area that you feel reasonably comfortable with and that you have more than just a vague, non-descript interest in. Here is an example: to choose to write on a Law of the Sea-related topic simply because it appears to be 'interesting' would be, for one who has never studied or worked in the field of Public International Law, to make a choice the merits of which would, in the best of cases, be debatable. If topics that you are largely (or entirely) unfamiliar with are 'no-go areas', topics you are attracted to from having been exposed to earlier in your life, whether as a student or as a professional, are those that you are most likely to be able to write something worthwhile about. 'Is that to say that one needs to be an area expert before one takes up postgraduate research studies on a topic chosen from that area?' I can imagine some of you wonder. Not at all: if anything, to want to know more about a subject that you are not entirely familiar with (but which is nevertheless not un-charted territory to you either) can provide the drive you will need to produce, through your sustained effort and commitment, a research degree-level piece of work, something that only a healthy measure of scientific curiosity can help you achieve.[21] However, as suggested earlier in this section, unless you have a reasonable command of the basic 'tools of the trade' in your field of research, choosing a topic from an area that you have previously had no (or very little) contact with can be a recipe for disaster of only marginally smaller proportions to the one that is likely to befall you if you choose an abstract or ill-defined topic, compromising, in the process, your chances for a timely completion of your work.[22]

A *third* rule of thumb is to choose, if possible, a research topic that relatively few others have inquired into (provided, of course, that this is not because there is nothing to be said about it). However counter-intuitive, that is, in fact, a very good starting point in your quest for a promising research topic. Writing about a topic that few others have addressed can certainly be a challenging task since there will be relatively little material that you can rely and build on so as to make your own substantial contribution to the field. However, little researched topics also present a number of significant advantages that make them worth considering. One is that your topic will, by definition, be an engaging one, both for you and your supervisors (that you will need to 'entice' into accepting to supervise your work and who are likelier to show interest in a more unconventional topic) and, later on, for your examiners or anyone else interested in your work. What is more, such a choice can also help you meet more easily the originality requirement for the award of your degree.[23] Another related advantage of little researched topics is that these are likely to afford your examiners less material that they can 'use against you' in your *viva* (i.e. in the defence of your thesis): if, by the time of your oral examination, you have become, through your effort and the time you have invested writing your PhD, *the* area expert, in a 'virgin' area no less, the likelihood is small that there will be many knowledgeable people around to challenge your conclusions (and, *in extremis*, to fail you) provided, of course, that your conclusions are plausible and robust enough to withstand *bona fide* criticism. Moreover, if you propose publishing some of your research work, whether during your research, in the form of an article, or after its conclusion, in the form of a book, what you will find is that an original research topic is easier to get journals or publishers interested in compared to a more 'run-of-the-mill' topic, helping you gain more visibility and recognition in your field of research (and, possibly, a modest source of income while you are at it).[24]

On the importance of a candidate's choice of topic in terms of the wider recognition of their research work (and of their hard-earned doctoral title, once their work is complete) the reader may care to note the following. As this author has argued earlier in this section, your enthusiasm for a demanding research topic should be tempered by the realization that, ultimately, your key objective is to fulfil an academic requirement. Having said that, not every PhD is worth the same as any other PhD, even if both have been taken at the same School, or even under the same supervisor. A more standard topic will give you the same academic rights as a more innovative one: both authors will be Doctors in their respective field (or in the same field, as the case may be). But only one of the two will elicit, by virtue of their work, that additional touch of peer respect and recognition, which an 'exotic' topic carries with it.[25] *Choose your topic carefully and your choice will pay off in more than one ways; but do not aim too high if your scholarly aspirations are not to be defeated by the sheer demands of a less standard research topic.*

'Where will I find such an original, little researched but manageable topic?' I can hear some of you ask. There are two points you will need to take note of while trying to come up with an answer to what is, effectively, the 'million dollar question'. The first is that your past exposure to your research area of choice is likely to yield a topic that you suspect may not have been thoroughly investigated or in the context of which widely divergent views have been expressed by commentators and academics alike. Even if you think you 'know' that there is research potential in a given topic, you will need to systematically go through the extant literature to establish whether or not the novel topic which you (think) you have identified has not already been exhausted by your precursors (a topic which may sound novel to you need not necessarily be so). A meticulous review of the literature to help you test your assessment of the novelty, or otherwise, of a topic you believe you have identified or to discover aspects of a known topic that do not seem to have been addressed satisfactorily is an exercise that you will, in any event, need to invest time in *prior* to taking up your research work, for two reasons no less. The first is as an integral part of the process of choosing your research topic (a literature review being the safest means of ascertaining that the work that you propose undertaking is, actually, necessary, because there is a cognitive gap, a genuine issue to which no 'answer' is readily available and which you would propose providing through your research); the second is as part of preparing for the actual writing-up stage of your work (a critical literature review being likely to be part of your introductory chapter or chapters).

Another point for prospective candidates to keep in mind is that, in order for them to identify interesting topics, they will have to follow developments in the 'real' world: peruse professional association publications and academic journals, read news-papers, visit blogs, constantly be on the look-out for a novel or controversial (but not polemical)[26] topic and you cannot go wrong.[27] It is in those places that prospective candidates will have to look for ideas and that is where they are the most likely to find them. In particular, reputable newspapers and respectable blog-sites can be a surprisingly lucrative source of research ideas that should not *a priori* be dismissed as sources of inspiration, whether at the planning stages of one's work or thereafter, simply because they appear too 'popular' or 'unscientific'. Do not underestimate the *stimuli* that these can provide and their general utility as a source of information and ideas. 'Unconventional' sources such as the above can provide you with food for thought, which can be just as valuable as factual information, and often more.

In your quest for a manageable research topic with adequate PhD-potential, you are, needless to say, not entirely alone. Your prospective School is unlikely to offer you a place to study for a postgraduate research degree unless those responsible for the selection of appropriate candidates feel, on the basis of your research proposal, that your choice of topic (as well as the way in which you would propose developing it) fulfil certain minimum criteria. Having said that, even if Universities will, at the selection stage, put a brake on obviously vague or unsuitable research topics and although supervisors can, *ex post facto*, try to help you fine-tune the scope of your research, it is with you (and you alone) that the final responsibility for deciding upon a manageable research topic lies. As your choice of topic is a deeply personal matter, both your School and your supervisor could be excused for allowing you the benefit of the doubt, even if they are somewhat concerned as to the outcome of your endeavours, which is why your trust in the salutary role of their involvement in your ultimate choice of research topic should not be unreserved. What is crucial is that there should be no nagging doubt in *your* mind that your topic is one that you can handle. If in doubt, by all means reconsider your choice of topic while you still can!

Your choice of research topic is (or it should be) constrained by personal, intellectual and practical considerations. The ideal research topic is one that the candidate finds interesting and manageable, both conceptually and practically. Do not assume that your research topic will occur to you by serendipity or that you will pluck it out of thin air or that Divine Intervention will step in to lend you a helping hand, for it will not. Be alert and inquisitive and inspiration will, sooner or later, come. Once it has, you will need to seize the opportunity and translate it into a research proposal. The following section will explain how this is to be done, so that you can achieve your end-objective: complete your doctoral thesis in less than 3 years.

6. Translating your research topic into a thesis proposal

Whatever your choice of research topic, a sound research proposal will be a necessary complement thereto and a *sine qua non* condition for your admission as a research student as well as, in the long run, for your success in your doctoral thesis writing endeavour.

If identifying a good research topic requires a moment (or two) of inspiration preceded by a modicum of research and reflection, developing and translating that topic into an actual research proposal, a 'plan', a 'blueprint' or a 'roadmap' to guide you through your research, will require a good deal of perspiration.[28] This is the time for you to well and truly flesh out the main idea(s) underlying your research topic and determine, in as precise a manner as possible, the way (i.e. the sequence of steps) through which you would propose addressing them in your PhD thesis, even if the actual arguments and conclusions will have to wait for later. Here is the sequence of steps that this author would suggest that you follow:

- take an A4 sheet of paper (or two);
- write your research topic down, in the form of a doctoral thesis working title,[29] and elaborate on it through questions(apart from helping you test the logic of your assumptions and identify *lacunae* in the extant literature that your research can fill, these questions will offer early guidance on the possible answers to your core research questions, providing the draft headings of your doctoral thesis, as well as the raw material for your table of contents);
- organise your draft headings by 'conceptual

groups' and the ensuing groups will be the draft
chapters of your PhD thesis;

- revisit your skeletal research proposal on a
regular basis, whether in order to improve its
overall logic, readjust your headings or add
new ones that your research or reflections on
your topic have, in the meantime, shown to be
necessary (but which you had not thought of
originally) and, no less importantly, in order to
improve on its overall structure.

As you will discover later on, a comprehensive research
proposal should not only enable you to take stock of where
you are standing with your work, helping you monitor your
progress towards your end-objective: it should also form the
basis for a lot of your actual writing, which is why putting
together a substantial, rather than a sketchy, research proposal
and constantly updating it as your thinking matures and as
your research and writing continue are investments worth
making.[30]

For a practical example of what a thesis proposal will
look like you may want to draw inspiration from the skeleton
of this book, which is a work in the general area of 'PhD-
writing'; the author's 'research topic' (coinciding with the
title of this work) is 'How to write a PhD in less than 3
years'. To organise his work and explain how the objective
encapsulated in this book's title can be achieved, the author
has devised a number of questions: these are the headings of
this work. It is by adding the main arguments and some text
to each of these headings that, once he was past the stage of
reflecting on the 'roadmap' for his work, the author set out
to write (and did, eventually, write) this short book.[31]

It is only if you are happy that there are enough
(unanswered) questions to your research topic of choice (but
not too many, so that you can actually manage the work

that will inevitably be coming your way) or enough research questions to which there are more than one plausible answers that you can choose from that you can feel comfortable with your research proposal (and, by extension, with your research topic of choice). If the research questions are too few or the answers are obvious, chances are there is not enough in your hitherto ideas to help you write 100,000 words worth of text. In that case, without giving up, prematurely, on your research topic, you will need to think of ways to readjust the scope of your inquiry, adding more ideas or discussing, in more detail, your raw material.[32] If too 'shallow' a research proposal (in terms of the poor word-count that it can yield) can be problematic, too far-reaching a proposal should be no less of (and may well be even more of) a cause for concern. The reason is that too prolific a research proposal can, ultimately, prove unmanageable, exposing you to the risk of becoming overwhelmed by the sheer scale of the endeavour required to come to grips with its many different facets. If you are to be able to finish your doctoral thesis promptly you will constantly need to remind yourself, already at the planning stages of your work, of the need to keep your research questions down to a manageable level, weeding-out those which are too remote or too divorced, in conceptual or, no less importantly, in practical terms, from the main core of your research topic to deserve any of your attention or of your invaluable time.[33] If doing so means refining your research topic (in the sense of narrowing down its scope and avoiding side-issues) or, even, altogether abandoning it (but only as an *ultimum refugium*) so be it: you want to be able to finish your work sooner rather than later, remember?

It is also at this stage that you will need to decide not only what your research work *will* cover but, also, what aspects of your research topic you will *not* be addressing in your PhD thesis, leaving these to future work, for lack of relevance, space or, more importantly, expertise.[34] Clearly spell out your self-imposed limitations from the outset and make a point of sticking to them unswervingly, steering clear of promising but, ultimately, problematic side-issues that you are unlikely to be in a position to elaborate on in sufficient detail to be able to ward-off embarrassing questions at the time of your *viva*.

While the skeleton-building exercise is to be approached with an open-mind, what candidates need to take into account during the planning stage of their work is that of the many different ways of presenting its main building-blocks and of organizing the available evidence in order to demonstrate the points that they aspire to make in their thesis, only *some* will be sound enough to help them reach, in as straightforward, logical and rapid a manner as possible, a plausible conclusion. Others will entail painful detours and lengthy digressions which, apart from detracting from a candidate's objective of finishing her work in less than 3 years, are likely to confuse her supervisors and examiners and, possibly, the candidate herself. Opt for as simple and self- explanatory a research proposal as possible, avoiding tortuous constructions and obscure associations between one part of your work and another, trying to make sure that your every heading represents a stepping stone towards persuading readers of the validity of your 'thesis' and your chances will improve of achieving your end objective: finish your PhD in less than 3 years.[35]

7. On the importance of conclusions: 'putting the cart before the horse' or 'seeing light at the end of the tunnel'?

A brief word now on your conclusions (that should figure as the last entry in your proposal, however much left blank at this stage). 'Is it important that you have already reached, even if only roughly, a conclusion before your start your work, i.e. that you have arrived to an answer to your main research questions?' Well, yes and no.

Before embarking upon the arduous analytical work that your PhD thesis will be the end-product of you will need to develop a vision of your own about your research area, in general, and of your actual research topic, in particular. At the same time, you cannot exclude the possibility that your research may lead you to unexpected findings: it would be unfortunate that these should go to waste because of your preconceptions in terms of your desired conclusions or on account of a somewhat 'stilted' approach to your research work. What is interesting in the field of humanities and social sciences is that there can (and often will) be more than one truths: some times it will be equally possible to support one thing and its exact opposite without risking making logical jumps and unscientific value judgments, drawing unwarranted conclusions or advancing unfounded theories. What is important is that you choose your own truth, based on the available evidence, your perception of it, your ideas as an independent, free-minded agent and aspiring scholar, and that you marshal sufficiently robust arguments to support it, to present a new theory (even if this only contains a modicum of novelty) or to formulate a proposition of relevance to it and to reject another one as less plausible, as unworkable or as impractical. While your exact conclusion is something that you are highly unlikely to be in a position to foresee at the start of your research, it would help tremendously that you at least have some views about it (or that you feel that you are in a position to develop some, as you proceed with your research) since, as you will discover as you go along, these will affect the direction that your research will take, making you side instinctively with one version of the truth rather than with another. For instance, a conservative author is unlikely to be unreservedly against capital punishment, in the same way that a libertarian is likely to resent government intervention in the economic sphere. You do not need to consciously subscribe to any specific school of thought in order to harbour informed views or to have specific predilections: a reasonably educated, engaged person is bound to have such views and predilections, however subconsciously. These will inevitably have an impact on the direction that your research will take, also informing some of your conclusions. What you will need to ensure is that your views are constantly tested against the rigours of science and that your conclusions are objectively justified as opposed to being purely subjective and dictated upon you exclusively by non-scientific, value-based considerations or prejudices.

For an illustration of this last point look no further than in this book. The author's motivation for writing this short book was the firm belief (a 'preconception', if you will, however much justified by personal experience) that finishing one's doctoral thesis in less than 3 years is both possible and desirable. Drawing on his personal experience, he set out to explain, through the pages of this book, how this objective can be achieved. An essay in exactly the same area, that of PhD-writing, reaching diametrically opposed conclusions (namely, that writing one's PhD in less than 3 years is either undesirable or impossible or both) would be perfectly well conceivable and legitimate, provided that its author is in a position to adduce sufficiently robust arguments to persuade readers of his 'thesis'. Choosing between his truth and that of the author of the present work would then be a matter left to the discretion of their respective readership, in much the same way that examiners need not fail two candidates simply because they advance different conclusions in their thesis, provided that both works 'hold water' and are 'scientifically' adequate. The same should be true of your doctoral thesis, if it is to stand the test of *bona fide* academic criticism and if it is to help you achieve your ultimate goal: finish your PhD in less than 3 years.

A related (but different issue) is the following. Your research should, at all times, be *pro veritas*. It would be unethical and unscientific to conceal or to bend facts that do not support your views, to 'soft-pedal' over issues suggesting that there is another viewpoint, to gloss over logical inconsistencies in your reasoning (or in that of those of your precursors whose teachings you have chosen to follow) or to otherwise mislead the reader into assuming that there is no alternative to your approach or that your conclusions are unassailable. Your examiners are more than likely to see through such manoeuvring, even if your supervisor does not, and that can land you in trouble at the worst possible moment namely, during your *viva*.

8. Originality and substantial contribution

This brings us to our next two topics, those of 'originality' and of 'substantial contribution', both of which will prominently figure, and rightly so, in your University's academic regulations as requirements for the award of a PhD degree in your subject area.

Your doctoral thesis will only be worth the time and effort you will be investing to produce it if you can use it as a vehicle through which to express one, at least (but, preferably, more) *new* and *substantial* ideas. What 'substantial' stands for in this context is, more or less, clear: an idea that takes no more than a few pages to advance, develop and substantiate will not be 'substantial' enough for the purposes of your doctoral thesis (although it may well suffice for an article in an academic journal or for a conference paper). What amounts to an 'original contribution' to knowledge in your particular field and what threshold of originality a candidate needs to satisfy are, no doubt, more tricky questions.[36] They also represent stumbling blocks that, ever so often, put otherwise competent prospective candidates, with a good research potential, off the idea of taking up postgraduate research studies (allowing room for some less competent candidates, with a weaker critical faculty, to do so instead).

When looking at your research proposal, not in its individual details this time but as a whole, take a moment, if you will, to ask yourself and reflect on the following question: 'Am I contributing anything new to my proposed field of research?' Your research topic and the way in which you propose approaching it (both are important in their own right and can, even independently, fulfil the originality requirement) will only be worth your while if to that simple question you can provide the following simple and unequivocal answer: 'Yes, even if only modestly so.'

There is one major consideration for you to take note of here: a contribution to your proposed field of research need not necessarily be anything ground-breaking or world-shattering. You will not need to reinvent the wheel, to solve a lifelong mystery or to advance a theory that the Nobel Foundation will consider worthy of a prize.[37] What you *will* need to do is to take knowledge in the field of your research a small step forward. How does one do that? Using your main idea (or ideas) as a starting point, your task will be to piece-together and organize, in an intelligent and coherent manner, as much of the relevant 'evidence' as possible, to distil dispassionately, objectively and critically (mere descriptions will not do) the 'lessons' learned from it and, finally, to formulate a conclusion of your own, based on its examination, that is *materially* and *qualitatively* different from what is already in the public domain, whether because to the findings of your precursors you have added some of your own, based on original primary research and analysis you have conducted, or because your inquiry into the differences and similarities between the conclusions reached by your forerunners has revealed a 'pattern' that no one else before you had detected or explained or because you purport to apply their findings to a different and possibly novel phenomenon, with a view to finding out more about its nature and to charting its relationship to other, better known phenomena.

Although some choices of topic will help you achieve the 'originality' objective more readily than others (which is why, as this author has argued earlier in this book, a novel topic is not to be avoided, however daunting it may appear to be) a general rule of thumb is that for a candidate to assemble an argument that no one else before her has, in materially the same way, demonstrating, in the process, independent critical power, is to do enough to pass the test of originality. If the first researcher to attack an entirely new research topic or to comprehensively address an obscure aspect of a better established one will no doubt have achieved something (genuinely) original, the first one to approach a known topic from a different, more original perspective will also have fulfilled her originality quota. Novel but, seemingly, terse or uninteresting research topics are also conceivable and they can perfectly well serve your purposes: for example, if nobody else has conducted a comparative examination of the regulation of fruit markets in Europe, the first candidate to do so and to apply the findings of her research to support a proposition or hypothesis (e.g. that these are too strictly regulated or that a different regulatory focus would facilitate the convergence of regulatory standards, with benefits for the end-consumer) will have produced an original piece of research, however mundane or uninteresting their research may appear to be. Special, non-academic skills can be of use here: if you happen to be good with languages and can read academic writing published in different parts of the world, why not blend it together, trying to draw original conclusions from its comparative examination (e.g. as to the different perception, in different parts of the world, of the same phenomenon and as to the possible reasons accounting for these differences)? Whatever you do, do not allow yourself to be put off the idea of writing a doctoral thesis just because you are too modest or because you think you have nothing exciting to say.[38] More importantly, waste no valuable time trying to come up with the 'mother of all research topics'. *How* you will address your research topic is just as important as *what* that topic is; and less exciting topics are likely to be more manageable and easier to dispose of in a shorter period of time than more ambitious and demanding ones.

For a practical example of originality look no further than this book. Before taking up writing, its author had to conduct a mini market-research to determine whether or not there was room for (yet) another book in this field. It is only after realising that most of the available publications were contributions from professional academics, written mostly from the perspective of supervisors or examiners rather than from that of successful candidates *simpliciter*, that their contributions were too long (sometimes unnecessarily so) and not always very user-friendly (however much he could agree with a lot of what was in them), and that their approach was, sometimes, too 'scientific' to be accessible to the average candidate that he decided he would invest the time and effort necessary to produce this short book. It follows that, what makes this work an original contribution to the field is not the novelty of the topic addressed in its pages, as such (there are dozens of works on PhD-writing, some better than others) but, rather, its brevity, its practical approach, its simplicity and the background and motivation of its author. If you can achieve something similar in your proposed field of research, you will have passed the originality test with flying colours.

A final point you will need to take note of in this context is the following. 'Re-cycling' earlier research in your field for the purposes of your PhD thesis will not prejudice your claim to originality. Indeed, far from being objectionable, relying on previously published work is an integral part of the process of writing a doctoral thesis or any other major piece of writing, for that matter, such as a Masters' dissertation or an article in an academic journal.[39] As this author has argued earlier in this book, a good grasp of previous research and a sound understanding of the main issues in your field of research are amongst the *sine qua non* conditions for the successful conclusion of your work. This is because the scientific method you will need to apply for the purposes of your PhD-writing will involve taking your hypothesis as a starting point and collecting sufficient evidence to support it. The reason why you will need to come to grips with what others before you have had to say about your research topic is, therefore, so that you can avoid the trouble (and embarrassment) of 'reinventing' old ideas and, more importantly, so that you can build on ideas already in the public domain, synthesize them, detect any logical weaknesses or contradictions that these may hide and, most of all, divert them, in a scientifically sound and ethically inoffensive manner, to your own purposes, as arguments supporting your propositions and as evidence of the validity of your hypothesis.

On the evidentiary value of past research in the field of social sciences and humanities, what is important to keep in mind is that, however much you may disagree with them or question their premises, the views or findings of your precursors represent 'facts' that you will not need to independently verify before you can rely and build on them. Your task will be to refer your readers to the source of those views and findings so that they can verify the basis of your statements and determine what part of your doctoral thesis is an account of previous analysis and critical thinking and what part represents your own, original addition to what is already in the public domain in your field of research. Properly attribute past research and its use, far from challenging your claim to originality, will actually bolster it.

This is all there is to it and let nobody else tell you otherwise. Producing an original piece of work may not be easy; impossible, however, it certainly is not! The satisfaction you will derive from turning out an original piece of writing, within the meaning of this section, will, most certainly, be worth the effort, especially if doing so takes you less than 3 years.

9. A note on methodology

Finally, a note on research methodology, references to which abound in University regulations for the award of postgraduate degrees as well as in scientific journals and, inevitably also, in books on PhD-writing. That so much attention should be paid to methodology or that the adherents of different schools of thought in connection therewith should be locked in semi-religious wars of faith, as if convinced of the natural superiority of their preferred approach are phenomena that the author of this book admits to have never quite understood, at least not in the field of social sciences.[40] What is more, if there is, indeed, such a thing as a formalized research methodology for the non-positive science authors to follow, he is still unsure, some time after the successful completion of his research degree and the publication of his work in book format, what methodology he applied to his research work and, more importantly, whether or not his choice was a conscious as opposed to a 'natural' one, dictated upon him by common sense and the specificities of his topic rather than by any ideological *a prioris*.

Although candidates no doubt need to demonstrate *how* they have obtained their results and how they have arrived at their conclusions, so that their supervisors and examiners can verify them and better assess their merits, it remains the case that the products of critical thinking, robust argumentation and common sense defy strict methodological (or any other) categorisation. As a result, much of the debate surrounding methodology and its use can only be somewhat artificial, serving scholastic rather than academic interests, *stricto sensu*. Whilst hints at one's methodology or a general overview of the approach that one proposes taking in conducting her research are not altogether devoid of utility - serving as a 'map' of the methods utilized when researching and writing as lengthy and complicated a piece of work as a doctoral thesis - for a candidate to go as far as to provide exhaustive details on her methodology, striving to furnish a thorough description of how she went about collecting the necessary data as well as the analytical she used to draw conclusions based on it would, in this author's view, be a waste of time in the context of an endeavour where time is of the essence. Here is why.

A good piece of research writing, anyone will agree, has to combine a number of core features, whatever the methodology supposedly used for its production: it should be readable and comprehensible, it should advance an original idea or view and it should support them with sufficient evidence and coherent argumentation throughout, reaching a conclusion that reflects the contents of its analysis and which differs in some respects from those reached by the candidate's precursors, however much building on theirs. The production of such a piece of work requires careful planning, one or two main ideas, an element of novelty and originality and, most of all, painstaking drafting work (including constant revisions) to convey, as clearly and succinctly as possible, the author's perception of the issues addressed in her work. This is the universal recipe for good writing, whatever methodology one may think the author has applied to obtain her result. If all necessary ingredients are present and judiciously mixed, trying to artificially convince one's readers of the thoroughness of one's approach and of the soundness of one's methodology (for instance, through the inclusion of a chapter devoted to methodology) would, quite simply, be superfluous. What candidates need to remember is that it is not so much the methodology applied in any given context that counts but the result. A piece of writing that neatly fits into the 'doctrinal' or 'quantitative' analysis pattern but which is poor in terms of structure, weak in its analysis, unsound in its conclusions or otherwise inadequate will not be saved because of the methodology purportedly applied for its production: it will remain a substandard piece of writing, no matter what.

It is inevitable that the author of any well-considered piece of work will resort to comparisons, attempt to draw conclusions from differences and similarities in the treatment of an issue, draw on the teachings of other disciplines or deploy some quantitative and some qualitative analytical tools so as to develop her own theory about the subject matter of her inquiry or in order to substantiate her conclusions. But does any of the above single-handedly suffice to make her work fit in with the comparative, inter-disciplinary, quantitative, positivist, doctrinal or any other school of thought in terms of research methodology? Besides, however unsurprisingly, most decent pieces of writing will, as a matter of fact, balance several methodologies. Candidates will, for instance, need to tread a fine line between too much theory, possibly irrelevant to their research, and too little thereof, leaving readers in the dark as to the conceptual underpinnings of their work. Moreover, the exact mix of methodologies required to be followed for a given piece of work to be produced will vary, depending on its nature. Some work is more example-driven, while other work is more akin to positive science, involving the observation of one or more perceptible phenomena, followed by an attempt to figure them out and to devise a verifiable theory about them or to identify ways in which to resolve a specific issue. Good quality research work will combine some or even all of these different approaches. However that may be, to take time to 'formalise' one's research methodology concerns instead of devoting one's energy and resources to addressing the real issues arising from one's research would be a pure waste of time, in an endeavour where time is of the essence.

At the end of the day, the method you apply is only the means to an end, a tool that is to be used to achieve a result. That result is the one and only deliverable that counts. Call your work an example of 'integrated' or 'mixed' methodology, if you have to (mainly in order to deflect any scholastic criticisms) and draw a line there. Enough said on methodology.

PART II
PRACTICAL CONSIDERATIONS I
THE APPLICATION STAGE

10. Choice of supervisors and ongoing relationship

However solitary an endeavour, PhD-writing is a supervised activity: for better or worse you are not entirely alone in its pursuit. Depending on the area of your proposed research, you will typically be assigned one main and one second (auxiliary) supervisor, which you can already designate at the time of your application for admission at your School of choice. The tasks of your supervisors will be to provide expert knowledge in your field of research, even if not necessarily on your actual research topic (see infra), to comment constructively on your drafts and, ultimately, to encourage you to become an independent thinker. In the author's experience, your interaction with your second supervisor is likely to be minimal, in the absence of unforeseen circumstances. Whilst your main supervisor is, therefore, likely to be your only supervisor, for all intents and purposes, most of the author's advice in this section applies to your choice of both your main and secondary supervisor.

Your choice of supervisor will be amongst your most critical decisions as you prepare to undertake postgraduate research studies, both because this is a choice that is bound to carry a good deal of weight in your choice of University (you will want to apply for admission to the School of which your preferred supervisor is an academic member of staff) *and* because it will inevitably have an impact on the successful and timely completion of your work: indifferent, inexperienced or obstructionist supervisors are likely to develop into a source of constant frustration for the students they supervise, to the point of putting some of them off the idea of completing their work. For all its importance, this is one of the most difficult subjects to address in general terms, mainly because *subjective* factors will have a significant role to play in your choice. What the author's modest experience nevertheless suggests is that there *are* a certain number of 'dos' and 'don'ts' that one would benefit from following.

The author would, first of all, encourage you to choose, whenever possible, someone high-ranking within your University of choice to act as your supervisor. Do not be intimidated by the fact that he or she may be tenured professors. These, as you will discover, are far less likely to antagonize you compared to younger academics with 'something to prove', whether to others or to themselves. Younger, more enthusiastic academics can be more energetic and 'fun' to be around but, at the same time, they are likelier than not to be possessed of a more competitive frame of mind, which will often be inversely proportionate to their seniority within academia. You do not want to be arguing with them endlessly or, *a fortiori*, to be writing papers for *them* or to be doing *their* research: remember, every minute of your time counts and you need to be able to use it so as to come closer to achieving your goal which is to finish your doctoral thesis in less than 3 years. Moreover, the author would not necessarily encourage you to choose as your supervisor an academic who is *the* expert in your research subject. It is sufficient that the person you choose is reasonably conversant with the area of your research and can grasp the basics of your topic so as to be in a position to provide useful, informed common-sense guidance. If anything, to choose a subject expert to act as your supervisor could be a bad idea: you do *not* want a supervisor who would rather see you defend exactly the same position as he or she may have taken on this particular or any other, closely related topic in the course of their career, rather than develop your own ideas.

What you do want, instead, is to be left alone to develop

your own thoughts and to make your own deductions, backed by sufficient evidence to make them plausible and defensible, with your supervisors commenting thereon rather than steering you in the direction of their own ideas. What you also want is a supervisor who (i) is active in research (i.e. who publishes frequently in refereed journals and/or takes part in international conferences) and (ii) is herself the holder of a PhD, with first-hand experience of what it is like to be on the receiving end of a supervisor's advice and support (or the lack of them). Inactive academics are unlikely to be of very much help to you, whether as a source of inspiration or as a very reliable arbiter on what is a good and what is a less good piece of writing, by contemporary academic standards.

How should a PhD applicant go about evaluating a prospective supervisor's suitability and personal qualities? An inquiry into your prospective supervisor's research profile and publications record should suffice to give you an idea of their academic interests, an insight into their views and the extent to which these broadly correspond to yours and their overall academic presence. Your prospective supervisor's University webpage should contain sufficient information for you to draw some conclusions in these respects, helping you eliminate some academics and short-list others for the purpose of reaching a final decision.

On your prospective supervisor's *personal qualities*, the author's advice is that you freely and openly discuss your proposed choice of supervisors with as many of your prospective School's staff members as possible. Ask around to find the appropriate supervisors, both in terms of expertise and, more importantly, in terms of character, and see if they are recommended by different people for substantively the same reasons. Academics who are generally viewed as reasonable, pleasant and easy to work with are unlikely to turn out to be very different from their reputation once you have started working under their supervision (unless, of course, your conduct has anything to do with their change of tune). By the same token, you can safely assume that academics who are not too warmly recommended are to be avoided for a reason. You may well turn out to be the only person in the world that a fastidious, 'ivory tower' academic will get along with but, let us face it, the odds are against it, so do try to steer clear of them so as to minimise the risk of finding out the 'hard way' why it is that their peers are less-than-enthusiastic about them.

Once a candidate has chosen her supervisors and these have been appointed to supervise her work, there are three important things for her to keep in mind as regards her ongoing relationship with them.

The *first* is that your supervisors are *neither* your co-authors nor your copy-editors: they are your supervisors, no more and, hopefully, no less. Your supervisors will, no doubt, read your work, make corrections and suggestions for improvements, propose that you investigate angles that you may have overlooked, re-adjust subtly the emphasis or the balance of your work and, ultimately, invite you to reflect critically on your reasoning or conclusions. However, it is *you* who is holding the pen and it is exclusively *your* responsibility to decide *what* you want to write about, *how* you intend to go about doing it, *how* long you will take doing it and *what* you want your conclusions to be. Your success is yours and so is your potential failure, however well or badly these may reflect on your supervisors and however much the latter may have an interest in seeing you finish your work sooner rather than later, so that neither their own personal reputation nor that of their School (in terms of its PhD completion rates) suffer.

The *second* thing to keep in mind is that your supervisor

is likely to be someone busy (perhaps *very* busy, especially if they supervise more than one students at the same time or if their interests extend beyond academic teaching or tutoring). If you are going to get along well with them you will need to constantly remind yourself of the scarcity of their time and of the many competing calls on it and avoid, at any cost, to waste it unnecessarily. Keep regular contact, to remind them of your existence and to reaffirm your commitment to seeing your research project through. The best way to do so is by holding a physical meeting with them at least twice per term, to discuss your work with them. At the same time, be discrete and respectful of their limited time and patience by making a point of only requiring their attention once you have finished a substantial piece of writing that you want them to look into and discuss with you. To discuss your ideas with them *in abstracto* serves, more often than not, no useful purpose. Indeed, what you are likely to find out is that a general discussion with your supervisor to which you go unprepared, without first having taken the time necessary to organise and commit your thoughts to paper, might confuse as opposed to enlightening you. Take your time (but not too long) to formulate your own thoughts *and* to put them down in paper once they have matured in your mind, *before* you bother your supervisor with them. Give your supervisor sufficient time to reflect on what you have produced in writing and only then discuss your work with them, asking them for comments and for specific observations on your submission.

The *third* thing you will need to keep in mind is that, if you are going to get along well with your supervisors, you will need to build a good working relationship with them, engaging with them no more than is absolutely necessary for the purposes of your work and keeping a respectful distance from them in all other respects.[41] While a good working relationship takes two to establish, there is a lot that *you* can do to help bring it about. A studious, respectful and punctilious candidate is bound to go down well with her supervisor(s) who will tend to approach her as a colleague in the making rather than as a hopeless case. If you are to stand a chance of building that kind of relationship with your supervisors you will need to be punctual in the deadlines you have agreed upon with them for the delivery of written work, remembering to agree on your next deadline and on your next appointment every time you meet to discuss your work. It is only by keeping your part of the deal that you can hope both to make steady progress with your work and to keep the sort of contact with them that will not make them want to avoid you at any cost but, instead, look forward, with some interest, to your next draft, understanding the need to treat you and your work with the respect that your commitment and dedication deserve.

A solid working relationship with your supervisors is, therefore, of paramount importance, considering the academic input, constructive criticism and overall support that you can expect from them at every stage of the process leading up to the completion of your work. If your relationship should turn out to be impossible, despite your best endeavours, by all means ventilate your concerns, first with your supervisor and, then, if need be, through the appropriate channels in your School, requesting a replacement (main) supervisor if you feel you have to. Although the decision to change your supervisor is one that you should not take lightly,[42] to suffer in silence is not a very good idea, especially where no realistic prospect of improvement is in sight. Your suffering can come at the cost of unnecessary aggravation and delays that you are well advised to avoid if you are to achieve your objective: finish your PhD thesis in less than 3 years.

11. Choice of School, reference letters and application

One of the main issues that you will need to address at the application stage is which School you will be registering with for the purposes of your postgraduate studies. Your choice of University will require some time and research, with the quality of each School depending on several factors, not all of which are easily measurable and not all of which are equally important for each individual candidate. Suffice it nevertheless to make the following general points on your choice of School.

Your choice of supervisor will, to a great extent, determine your choice of School. A knowledgeable supervisor who can help you through the PhD-writing process (be it only by not 'throwing spanners in the works') carries more weight than an Ivy League School with a less accommodating (or downright conceited) supervisor. This is not to say that one or more reputable, respected and recognizable Schools should not figure amongst your list of choices. However, your doctoral thesis will not count for (considerably) less because you have undertaken it in 'X' as opposed to in 'Y' University; your research topic, how you develop it and who your supervisors and examiners are can be infinitely more important compared to your School. Moreover, what you are likely to find is that you can sometimes get more support and a better level of supervision in a not-so-well-known School (whose academic and administrative staff is more motivated) than you can hope to get at a University appearing higher up in the League Tables (which you should, in any event, take with a pinch of salt, as a personal visit can often be far more illuminating and eye-opening compared to an impersonal and, possibly, self-serving third-party assessment). The author's advice is, therefore, that, while you should aim high, you should be prepared to settle for second best if it is good enough and if your proposed supervisor meets your expectations (besides, there is hardly any room for all of us at Oxbridge).

A School you are already familiar with from your previous studies should, obviously, figure amongst your list of target institutions: it does not matter that you have been there previously, nor will this look bad on your *curriculum vitae*. Nobody will do you any favours and, if gaining admission is likely to be somewhat easier at a School where you are less of an unknown quantity, walking away with your degree will not be (you will, after all, be assessed in your *viva* by external examiners).

Finally, topographic considerations should also play an important role in your final choice. Especially if you will need to travel to meet your supervisor or to attend research seminars (for instance, because you are working full-time while writing your PhD, as the author did) you may find that a School that is within easy reach is preferable compared to one where the supervisor or the School appear to be marginally better but which you cannot reach without investing several hours (not to mention material resources) to travel.[43]

Once you have chosen a place to study you will need to apply for admission to it. Whatever your final choice of School, do make sure you apply early enough for admission. To avoid disappointment, apply at least six months in advance or preferably as early as one full year before you propose taking up your postgraduate research studies. You would not want a prospective supervisor that you have taken great pains to identify to have no spare capacity for you at the time of your application!

Applying for admission will, *inter alia*, involve obtaining reference letters and submitting a research proposal. First, a word on reference letters. If you have been outside academia for some time, you may find this, of all PhD application requirements, to be the most daunting, so much so that you may even be tempted to altogether give up on the idea, frustrated that you risk never being given a chance to fulfil your research aspirations for not having access to reference letters.[44] A word of advice from the author's personal experience: do not be too shy or too coy. Knock on the door of your University teachers of 5 or 10 years ago, tell them what you are after and explain yourself as frankly and openly as you can. Some will say 'no', others will decline to help in a more polite or indirect manner, resorting to pretexts, some more plausible than others. But others will volunteer their help.[45] Show your commitment and make it work for you. Dare and you can win! If you cannot get hold of an academic reference, get one or more professional references from a member of staff with academic credentials from you place of work (preferably, someone familiar with your work). And remember to attach to your application to the University of your choice some written work, if you have any. That will prove the point you are trying to make: 'I am in a position to write a text, which will make sense to anyone reading it and which will comply with certain minimum academic standards.' That is what a prospective referee or your future School will want to see: somebody who will not be an embarrassment or a burden to them but who is likelier than not to add to their reputation, living up to their PhD-writing ambitions. What better documentary evidence can there be than a previous piece of writing?

One final point is worth making on a crucial part of your PhD application file, namely your research proposal. Do not underestimate its importance and do not make the mistake to treat it as just one of the several documents that you will have to provide as part of your application in order to gain admission at your School of choice. While each academic institution is likely to have its own concrete requirements in this regard, your research proposal should, effectively, consist of your skeletal research proposal (the one this author has touched upon in section 6 of this book), setting out, as clearly as possible, your research questions and, depending on how advanced your reflections on your research topic are, some hints as to the possible outcome of your work. Your research proposal should also include (i) a concise literature review, identifying authors whose work is of relevance to your research topic (ii) a (brief) account of the methodological tools that you plan making use of in order to come up with answers to your research questions and (iii) details of your proposed timetable for the completion of your work. Take time to draft your research proposal as clearly and succinctly as you possibly can, making sure that you provide, for the benefit of its readers, answers to the following three questions: first, what research you plan to undertake; second, why your research is worth undertaking; and, third, how you intend to proceed with your proposed research. Not only will a solid research proposal guarantee you a place to study as a research student: as this author has argued in section 6 of this book, it will also serve during your studies as a blueprint, as a source of guidance through the maze of your research and as a point of reference for your work, when in doubt. Take the time required to get your research proposal right and your investment will stand you in good stead throughout the course of your PhD research and writing, hopefully helping you complete it in less than 3 years.

PART III
PRACTICAL CONSIDERATIONS II
THE RESEARCH AND WRITING STAGE

12. Researching and writing your PhD thesis

Now that you have chosen your topic, found two academics willing to supervise your work as well as a place to study you will need to start with your actual research and writing. This is where you go back to your research proposal and begin addressing, one by one, the questions you have identified there (and any other, closely related ones, that are bound to crop up in the course of your research). This section examines how candidates will need to go about writing their doctoral thesis, which pitfalls they ought to avoid and which principles they will have to internalise throughout the writing stage so as to complete their work promptly.

Contrary to what many might think, writing a PhD (or any other major piece of writing, for that matter) is not (or should not) be about endless hours of research into and of reading up on one's subject, followed by a few (or, in any event, fewer) hours of writing. It is (or should be) exactly the other way round. It is through writing that a candidate's ideas on their research topic will progressively mature, that the logic of their thoughts will be tested against the rigours of scientific research and that they will be accumulating words toward their final word-count requirement. To be able to write anything intelligent and coherent candidates will, obviously, need to read and reflect on what others before them have had to say on their subject; as this author has argued earlier in this book, familiarising oneself with the work of one's precursors will also keep them from wrongly assuming that they are being original or innovative in their research (only to discover, later on, much to their embarrassment, that others have been there first). But to reflect for hours on end on previous contributions without putting pen to paper is not a very productive way for candidates to use their precious time (nor does it augur very well for the future of their research endeavours): it is only through synthesising *in writing* what others before them have had to say about their subject,[46] through testing the logic of their arguments and conclusions, through detecting any inconsistencies or *lacunae* in the extant literature and, finally, through adding their own thoughts to what is already in the public domain (an exercise that, as we have argued earlier, need not involve rediscovering America) that candidates can hope to make progress towards achieving their end-objectives. Candidates should, therefore, resist the tendency of pouring-over and digesting thousands of pages worth of published research before they can write a single page of their own! Start writing from day one, if possible, and keep reading up and writing in parallel, until your work is finished (you will, eventually, finish, that much is guaranteed, if you follow this approach). Never mind if relatively little of what you write in the first three or four months will end up in your thesis: the experience, alone, you will be acquiring through the process of writing, the knowledge you will be accumulating and the expertise you will be developing, as a result, in your subject area are invaluable *per se* and well-worth the investment.

This takes us to the next crucial point for you to keep in mind. Contrary to what some might think, writing a PhD is not and should not be a part-time occupation (although you may be excused for thinking otherwise, judging from the offer of part-time research courses for working, mature students).[47] Because of the intensity of the PhD-writing task and of the effort, which candidates will need to put into it, especially if they do not intend to make of it an inordinately long exercise, research students cannot allow days or, *a fortiori*, weeks to go by without reflecting and, more importantly, without *writing* on their topic. What candidates will need to do instead - and if there is one piece of advice that the author would heartily ask you take from this short book then please let it be this - is to work on their PhD every single day, to the extent possible, treating their research as a regular job to which they will need to devote a, more or less, set number of working hours (even if they may have to be flexible as to *which* hours of the day these will be). There are several reasons why candidates will need to approach PhD-writing as a 'job'. The first is that long breaks in between productive spells are bound to disrupt a candidate's train of thought and her momentum. What long (or, even, not so long) pauses are likely to be accompanied by are memory lapses: candidates risk forgetting what they intended to say, why they intended to say it and what prompted them to go down this or that path in their research and writing. The author has found that places he left blank in his draft doctoral thesis with the intention of 'filling in later' (with an emphasis on footnote references) he almost invariably ended up forgetting all about.[48] Remember, therefore, to formulate complete (rather than elliptic) arguments and to record the details of all your references if you are to steer clear of the risks to which memory lapses are bound to expose you. A second reason why candidates cannot afford to take pauses is this: what one will discover, if one can stick to the proposed daily work discipline, is that every new day will bring one or more new ideas, a novel twist to one's hitherto thoughts, a subtle but cumulative improvement to one's evolving manuscript. Candidates cannot afford to loose a single day if they are going to see themselves making the steady progress necessary to ensure that they can finish sooner rather than later. Does that mean that your PhD has to monopolise every waking hour of your existence? Not at all. What it does, however, mean is that, save for *force majeure* situations, there should not be a single day when you do not do at least one or, preferably, many more hours worth of work on your PhD thesis. If you *have* to travel, print out your draft work (specifically, the part that you have been working on at the relevant time) to take along with you in the airplane or on the train: you will be surprised how many small (or not so small) errors or inconsistencies, logical or other, you will discover in what you thought was a finished piece of work or how many new ideas you will come up with while reflecting on your work.[49] If you need to be away from your desk but would rather not read through your drafts over and over again, why not read somebody else's work and reflect on any useful ideas that this may contain and how these could be incorporated into your draft thesis? Take an article along that you have printed out some time ago but never had an opportunity to read through or a book of relevance to your topic and leaf through it. Mark the relevant parts, those that support your thoughts and those that contradict them. Your options are endless. Whatever you do, try not to allow a single day to pass you by without devoting *some* of it to a pursuit of relevance to your PhD. Remember, this is not a part-time occupation and you want to be able to finish in less than 3 years.

Another common misconception of relevance to the writing stage of doctoral degrees that is worth dispelling is that a candidate's first year differs, fundamentally, from the second or third years of their research. The truth is that it does not or, better put, it *should* not, at least not if you are to complete your thesis promptly. While one's first year as a research student and the progress they can accomplish during that year will, to some extent, shape what is to follow, candidates would be ill-advised to assume that they can afford to spend the first twelve months of their doctoral studies 'reflecting' on their research topic (for instance, devoting it to a literature survey so as to better define the scope and the focus of her research topic). *Writing* is what a candidate will need to do, as of the earliest possible stages of her research studies (not least because a good deal of what a candidate writes in the first several months of her work will not find its way into her final draft) and writing is what a candidate will need to continue doing until she is through with her work. The specificities of your first year (and there are some)[50] should, therefore, not appreciably affect your routine or the manner in which you would propose approaching your work, which should involve primary research, analysis and writing from the first to the last day, to the extent possible. It follows that neither your attendance of research seminars (the dubious privilege of first year research students) nor your preparations for your transfer event[51]-- typically scheduled to take place at the end of the first year of your registration -- should detract from your research and writing routine. Your first year is, therefore, no 'trial year': it should, for all intents and purposes, be treated like any other year in your doctoral degree writing struggle and it is your call whether this will be one of only two or, instead, three, four or more years that you will be spending researching and writing your doctoral thesis.

The next important consideration for candidates to keep in mind is that, if they are to be successful in their PhD-writing endeavours with the least amount of effort, they will need to decompose their work in smaller, manageable work-parcels, disposing of each one of them in turn. It follows that you should think of your doctoral thesis as if consisting of more or less isolated 'compartments', capable of standing alone (for instance, as articles in a scientific journal). The benefit of dividing your work in smaller parcels and of conceptualising your doctoral thesis as if consisting of separate but interrelated entities that logically follow from one another is that you can hope to manage these more easily than you can hope to manage a more substantial piece of work where the risk of losing your sense of direction is bound to be considerably more substantial. The human mind is, after all, a processor. The lucky few can exercise command over the entire field and play around with ideas across the canvas of their work, much like the great Renaissance painters could. The rest of us have to think 'smaller' if we are not to be overwhelmed by the scale of an enterprise as demanding as PhD-writing. If you can achieve that (and this will, to a great extent, depend on the quality of your skeleton), you are likely to be pleasantly surprised in three different ways. *First*, you will be able to finish your work quicker than you ever could if this were to consist of two or three chapters only, gaining in confidence as you progress with your work. *Second*, it will be easier for you to display a logical progression in your thinking, from one chapter to the other, one that your examiners and supervisor can follow through and that you can rely on when working (at the very end of the process) on your abstract and introduction.[52] Finally, what you will find is that free-standing pieces of work are easier to publish in a journal, whether prior to finishing your PhD thesis or thereafter, compared to bigger and less manageable pieces. Journals do not welcome very long pieces, unless you are well known and respected in the field. The likelihood that you are either or both of these things if you are reading this book is small.[53]

Finally, a few words on your writing schedule and on the sources of your inspiration. Starting with your schedule, the time will be ripe for you to reflect on and set a timetable for your future work immediately after you have produced your 'roadmap'. Set shorter and longer-term goals and use your best endeavours to stick to them, avoiding procrastination. Plan your days and weeks ahead as carefully as you possibly can. Make at the end of each day a list (be it only a mental one) of what you will need to look into the day after, while today's thoughts and challenges are still fresh in your mind.[54] Be realistic in your goal-setting but, at the same time, demand no less than what you are in a position to deliver, internalising the prospect of having to go the extra mile in order to be able to finish your work sooner rather than later. Factor in time that you will be unable to work on your doctoral thesis either because it is Christmas Eve and you will need to spend time with your family or because it is your best friend's birthday or because you may be unwell or for any other reason that cannot, reasonably, be avoided whether or not it can be foreseen. A plan of three months for a 35 page-long draft chapter of around 18,000 words, including footnotes, is, in the author's experience, realistic. Remember: a full first draft is a very important milestone, representing an achievement in itself! It is only once you have such a draft that you can refine it, improve on it, reflect on its weaknesses and merits and, most of all, share it with your supervisors for their comments and feedback. It is only then that you can afford to feel at ease with your work, confident that you can finish the task you have undertaken in the time that you have allocated to it, and, no less importantly, that you can expect to be taken seriously by your supervisor, 'conditioned' to expect to hear from you on a regular basis and to have to provide feedback to your work.[55]

Regarding your sources of inspiration (i.e. the raw material for your work) the following thoughts (in addition to those formulated in section 8 of this book) are apposite. While you should no doubt consult traditional sources of information, including textbooks, journals, specialised databases and, possibly, relevant theses you will be surprised to discover how much of what you need for your research is, literally, at your fingertips. Sit in front of a computer with an internet connection and you will soon find that, within split seconds, you can have access to a good deal of the materials that you will end up using for your work, whether for its literature review section (assuming that you have one) or for other aspects of your doctoral thesis. Do not underestimate, therefore, the potential of the new technologies: they can save you time, effort and resources. The author often found himself wondering how much more difficult his work would have been if he had to physically consult many of his sources and, literally, drinking to the health of the insightful people behind several of the better known search engines (at least one of which has a branch specifically dedicated to scholarly work). Two words of caution are apposite here. *First*, while it is true that there is a lot of material, which reputable academic journals, think-tanks, institutions and other *fora* have made available electronically, in PDF format or otherwise, and which you can rely on as you would on a hard copy version thereof that you would hope to find at your School's library, there is also a lot out there in the brave new world of the internet that is inaccurate, unreliable or downright wrong. So, beware. *Second*, the ease with which you can access information through the internet can prove a blessing and a curse if, as a result, you end up suffering from 'information overload': choose your sources carefully and remember to exercise restraint on your academic greed for endless amounts of material that you would, in any event, be unable to process, at least not without detracting from your goal, which is to finish your doctoral degree in less than 3 years.

13. Other issues and practical tips for the research and writing stage

What follows is a list of essential 'Dos' and 'Don'ts' that you will need to internalise while working on your manuscript. Make a point of sticking to the author's advice and the result will reward your efforts, hopefully in less than 3 years.

a) Back up your work with authority: However 'interesting' sounding, unsubstantiated statements and arbitrary, fanciful conclusions are unscientific and they can cause you embarrassment. You cannot be plucking conclusions out of thin air or be expounding ideas that are not the culmination of a thinking process charted by your research work and premised on a review of what learned scholars in your area have had to say about your research topic (or specific aspects of it). Whilst in order to produce a good doctoral thesis you will not necessarily need to discover the *one* scientific truth nor prove every point you are making beyond the shadow of doubt, what you *must* do, if you are going to be successful in your PhD-writing endeavour, is to choose your own truth and to present it in a plausible, robust and intellectually rigorous manner. Remember, there are more than one ways to approach your subject and more than one legitimate conclusion (at least in the fields of arts and humanities). It does not so much matter *what* your conclusion is: what *does* matter is that yours is backed by authority, that it sounds plausible and that it is not akin to a house of cards, ready to collapse at the first gust of wind. Where you are proposing something genuinely new, backing it with authority will not always be possible. But, even then, your assumptions will have to follow from your research and they should be grounded on the findings of scholarly research work of relevance to yours.

b) Be fair with the work of others before you: Do not forget to always acknowledge your precursors' work in your PhD thesis, whether or not you quote directly from their work (in which case plagiarism may also be an issue – see *infra*). This is a *sine qua non* ethical requirement and there may well be sanctions foreseen in your School's rules for failing to do just that. Do not be put off the idea of acknowledging the work of other scholars and including proper citations to their work merely because that would entail inserting a good deal of footnotes to your draft. There is absolutely nothing reprehensible about footnotes containing references to scholarly publications; nobody expects you to single-handedly devise everything that your doctoral thesis will contain but, instead, to build on existing knowledge, thoughts or ideas in order to produce your own, original piece of research. When relying on your precursors' work, remember to do so in a fair manner. Do not take statements or thoughts out of context. First get a reasonably good idea of what other scholars are on to and only then include references to their work in your thesis. If you happen to disagree with something or everything of what they have said, avoid sweeping your disagreement under the carpet or glossing over it or, *a fortiori*, deriding them for holding views opposed to yours. Remember that yours is a scientific piece of work that should present both sides of the argument. If you are pro-death penalty and somebody else is against, try to bring logical inconsistencies in their reasoning to surface, see if theirs is a minority view or if there is some measure of bias that can help explain away views, which you consider flawed or illogical. Your research work has to be *pro veritas* and your examiners will appreciate seeing opposing views in your thesis as indications of a thorough literature review and of a quest for as global a presentation as possible of the extant thinking on your research topic.

c) Steer clear of plagiarism: The temptation to plagiarise, defined as the *verbatim* use (or very close imitation) of the language[56] used by another for the formulation of thoughts and its passing-off as one's own original work will, understandably, be great, especially if you feel drained or if you are not a native speaker and would rather borrow the language used by another to formulate specific thoughts rather than come up with your own. One word of advice: however strong the temptation to plagiarise, never, ever, ever fall for it. It is unethical and, should you be discovered (which you will) you risk embarrassment and, perhaps, much more.[57] Plagiarism, it is worth noting, is akin to a ticking time-bomb. Plagiarists have been discovered decades down the line and, in some cases, stripped of their academic titles or professional privileges, much to their discomfort. You do not want to live in fear nor do you want to risk being discredited by making false claims of authorship, detrimental to your integrity and reputation (not to mention to that of those whose language and ideas you have borrowed without due attribution). If your motivation for plagiarism is a weakness in language rather than a paucity of ideas, try to get your work edited by a professional, brush up your language skills, seek the advice and help of a native speaker in formulating your thoughts or test them on the internet for grammar, punctuation and their consistency with English usage. Whatever you do, never, ever, ever plagiarise!

d) Link different parts of your work through internal cross-references and constantly check the logical structure and narrative flow of your draft: If your work consists of distinct parcels, as this author has argued that it is preferable that it should, you will need to provide 'bridges' that your supervisor, examiners and readers (should you later wish to publish your work) can use to walk through your reasoning. To achieve that, use conclusions and introductions in each chapter of your work as well as cross-references throughout to previous or to following parts of your draft. Doing so will not only help you guide your readers through your work and shepherd them to your conclusion/s; it will also help you overcome the risk that the different parcels of which your work consists do not logically cohere or that there are inconsistencies between one part of your draft and another. It is only if one proposition logically follows from a previous one, in a more or less uninterrupted manner, and if there are no internal inconsistencies that you can feel secure in the product of your intellectual labour. It serves no purpose writing six chapters,[58] which, if seen in isolation (for instance, as free-standing articles in an academic journal), are brilliant if one or more of them are contradicted by the other, even in details, or if they do not logically follow from one another. Your examiners are bound to pick up potential inconsistencies and embarrass you unnecessarily during your *viva* or demand corrections if they are going to decide that you have been (conditionally) successful. The structure and coherence of your work are of vital importance to your success: everything you say must serve your main underlying argument and lend support to it, preparing the reader for your final conclusion.

e) Mind your language: No matter what your subject area is, you will need to constantly remind yourself of the need to be cautious with the language used in your manuscript. While you do not need to have Shakespeare's language skills to write a PhD thesis, it is worth remembering that a well-written text, one whose author has taken the time to polish in terms of language, will not fail to impress. Successive approximations will, no doubt, be necessary if a decent result is to be achieved. Carry a red pen with you and go over your work at the end of each day (or at the start of the day after). There is always room for improvements in your style and clarity and in the manner in which you convey your ideas. Moreover, while good language skills cannot hide a paucity of ideas, it is often the case that a well drafted text is one which is likelier than not to convey well considered ideas. Avoid, at all costs, slang or unduly informal language: its use will not make your text more easily accessible, it will make it plain unscientific and that you will need to avoid. Use of the personal pronoun is also to be avoided: as your authorial claim over your work is guaranteed, you will not need to constantly remind, through use of the personal pronoun, those reading it that the ideas expressed in it are yours.

If informal language is to be avoided, so is unduly pretentious, pompous or convoluted writing. Those using it might think they will impress their examiners; chances are they will achieve quite the opposite effect. A related but somewhat different point is this: contrary to what you might think, a good quality thesis is not one that only you or somebody well versed in the intricacies of your particular field of research can understand, whether because of the ostentatious use of complicated jargon and technical language or because of the obscurity of your style or on account of the fogginess of your messages. Unnecessary complexity and lack of clarity (especially when intentionally pursued, whether or not as a screen for weaknesses in your reasoning) are not a plus, they are a minus. The hall-mark of a good text is in the ability of the average, non-sophisticated but reasonably educated reader to understand it, to follow its logic through and to draw a more or less clear conclusion as to what its author is on about. It serves no purpose to think up the most brilliant ideas if you cannot (or will not) express them in an intelligible and comprehensible manner and it is even more of a shame to forego plain language for the sake of impressing the examiner or the reader (who are unlikely to be impressed and are far likelier to be displeased for having to make additional effort to understand you and to follow your arguments through to their logical conclusion). Be particular about your use of language; read your text over and over again to detect and correct stylistic mistakes, improve on the language, weed out repetitions and smooth out its style and the result will, no doubt, reward your efforts.

f) Save your work: Imagine the following scenario. You have taken three months, or so, to write a draft thesis chapter. You have worked with the cool, professional enthusiasm that this book has recommended as the way to go. You have done your research, committed your ideas to paper, and polished the language and, all of this, at the price of not being able to join your colleagues on that wine-tasting trip to Hungary. You have had to spend your weekends at the library or at home, in front of your computer, instead of being outdoors, enjoying the good weather. You are one step short of putting the finishing touches to your work and sending it over to your supervisor as you had agreed. And then, disaster strikes: your computer breaks down and never again reboots. Your work is lost. Or, to make this even more dramatic, your laptop is lost at the airport or stolen from your University digs, or your room-mate spills coffee all over it or your parent's place burns and you computer becomes a fire casualty. Whatever the details of the disaster affecting your loyal doctoral thesis companion, the result is the same: your work is lost and all your investment in time and effort goes up in smoke. Even if you had read your text over a hundred times and even if your memory is brilliant, you will never be able to reproduce your laboriously crafted text out of memory. Some of your ideas will be lost forever and, while you may well be able to write an equally good replacement chapter, a good deal of your effort will have been lost for good, your writing schedule will have been upset and your morale will have been dealt a very serious blow indeed. Besides, do not assume that your supervisors will necessarily believe any of the above stories, adding insult to injury. What can you do to avoid a catastrophe of the above proportions befalling you? Well, it is simple: all you need to do is to save your work in back up files every single day! Name the files by date and save them in a USB stick (the author used two) that you carry along (separately from your computer, if that is a portable one). An additional precaution (which is by no means meant as an alternative to the maintenance of back-up files) is to print out and save the most recent drafts of each of your thesis chapters. It is a good idea to save your work chapter by chapter and, only at the concluding stages, merge them into a single document. Larger files can accelerate breakdowns, corruptions or other technical glitches that you are better off without. Even if you take all of these precautions you are bound to loose some of your work. But it will only be small parts thereof (the last 15 minutes of your work or so) that you can afford to loose and replace without any major ramifications. It is a fact of life that computers are fallible, for all their sophistication. Save your work every single day and store your back up files and print-outs in a safe place!

g) Sequence of writing: A PhD (or any major piece of writing, for that matter) is only seldom (if ever) written the way your examiners or audience will read it. Do not make the mistake to assume that you need to necessarily follow the sequence of your research proposal when writing your thesis (this book was not written in the sequence you are reading it either; the same was true of the author's PhD thesis). You do not need to (nor are you likely to be able to) draft your individual pieces in the sequence that these will appear in the final product; indeed, what you are practically guaranteed to find as you go along is that what you thought should come first can only be tackled last. As you will realise while progressing with your work, its conceptual part (which, in your final manuscript, will almost invariably precede the descriptive component of your work) can only be sensibly written *after* you are done describing your research topic. This, if one should think about it, only makes sense. Let us think of an example: to decide what the regulatory rationale for a certain activity should be (a question to which there is a *why* and a *how* sub-question) you need to describe that activity first, so as to see what distinguishes it from other activities, what makes it similar to other, already regulated activities and what conclusions of relevance to your research question can be drawn from that. The same is true of literature reviews which are, essentially, descriptions and distillations of what others have had to say on a topic and which are to be found in the introductory chapters of many a PhD theses. Thus, a rule of thumb to help candidates decide on the sequence of their writing is this: describe (or define) first and dissect only thereafter (even if, in a candidate's final product, the sequence in which one's work will be presented will be reversed). This, incidentally, is something that will help you progress with your work more expeditiously: descriptive pieces are, in principle, easier to draft compared to analytical or conceptual pieces, meaning that, if you do start with them, your task will be somewhat easier and you will not only manage to finish a large part of your work but, also, gain a good grasp of your research topic in the process, furthering your understanding of its particulars. This knowledge will stand you in good stead in your later research into the more demanding parts of your project, enabling you to 'kill two birds with one stone'. A related but different issue is that of deciding *which* part of your thesis a specific sub-issue should be addressed in. What you will discover is that, *in extremis*, as much as an entire draft chapter will have to be moved to a different part of your PhD thesis, so as to improve the narrative flow of your work and facilitate the reader's understanding of the mental process that led you to your conclusions (the all important 'moving of the furniture', as the author's supervisor used to put it).

h) When is your work over? Nothing in this world is ever perfect and improvements are always possible to practically everything. As you will discover as you progress with your work, writing your doctoral thesis is about revising time and again your drafts, correcting and improving on them, rationalizing them, deciding that a specific part fits better in this rather than in that place and so forth. The author filled several box-files with drafts before he was satisfied with the result and he was to be seen dragging along and marking the latest draft of the Chapter he was working on in trains, airplanes, trams and so on. However, if relentless revisions are an absolute must, what you will need to remember is that your time is not unlimited, nor is the space you have to expose your ideas in, for that matter. Perfection is subjective and, ultimately, unattainable. No matter how many times one has combed through a text, improvements, however minor, will always be possible. If one decides to publish one's work what one will realise is that right until the 11th hour minor errors, inaccuracies or stylistic points can be detected that one will want to correct or improve on, but which one had not picked up earlier. There is a word limit to your thesis (typically standing at around 100,000 words, depending on the discipline) and you will ultimately have to avoid overshooting it by wanting to write more or to update and enrich your text with additional ideas that occur to you or information that becomes available after you are done with a draft chapter of your thesis. However, you will need to decide at some stage that your work is over if you are not to risk never completing it, whether in less than 3 years or longer. The author's experience is that you will instinctively know when the moment is right for you to call it a day. It is when you are well and truly fed-up with re-working your manuscript that you know the moment is right for you to put the pen down. Ask yourself if you are genuinely saturated with your thesis or if you only *think* you are because you want to be over with it. It is only if you are confident that it is the former that you can safely declare victory and submit your work for examination. It is precisely in order to avoid the risk of revisiting your work *ad infinitum* that you need to work towards a final deadline and avoid postponing the completion of your research and writing. Stick to your timetable, trust your gut feeling and you cannot go wrong!

14. Publishing your work as you go

Taking sound advice, you have divided your work in manageable parcels and you are well under way with it, using every single day available to register progress towards the achievement of your objectives. Is there anything else you should or may want to do? As it happens, there is *one* thing that can be useful (however much it need not be necessary, as such). This is trying to publish some of your work while you are still working on your PhD thesis. 'Will that not take time out of my time, holding me back and disrupting my writing schedule?' I can imagine some of you wonder. There is no black or white answer to what, no doubt, is a legitimate question. But there are some advantages to publishing (some of) your work as you go, which is why this author believes firmly that doing so is not, necessarily, a bad idea, provided that your School allows it and that your supervisors have no objections to it.

Publishing externally requires time and effort, there are no two ways about it. This is especially so if your intention is to publish papers on 'side-issues' rather than to transform some of your research work into external publications. However, if you have followed the author's advice, dividing your work in manageable parcels, which can be disposed off less laboriously but, also, 'recycled' in a relatively limited amount of time into external publications, and if you have stuck closely to the subject matter of your research topic (rather than veered off to examine side-issues, not of the essence to your research topic) what you will discover is that the time and effort you will need to 'repackage' some of your thesis for external publication, whether in a journal or as a conference paper, will not be that significant.

There are at least three distinct reasons why you may want to consider trying to get (some of) your work published prior to finishing your doctoral thesis and, preferably, in time for your *viva*. The *first* one is that, in the vetting process leading up to your work's publication in a peer-reviewed journal, you are likely to receive input from the external publication's undisclosed referees or editor (or from the conference participants), complementing that of your supervisors, who may not have detected all possible areas of improvement in the work you have submitted for their comments. Any help you can obtain from any source to enhance the fruit of your labour, elevating it from a good to a very good draft, is worth the investment. If, on the other hand, you should receive the thumbs up but *no* comments (although the journal is a refereed one) then it must be because your work meets fairly high academic standards, which would no doubt be reassuring! Conversely, if your draft were to be rejected (or if its reception from the other conference participants should not be the warmest possible), you should perhaps be put on enquiry.[59] The *second*, no less important, reason why publishing some of your work as you go may be a good idea is because going public with your thoughts and findings in a suitable *forum* will enable you not only to become more widely known[60] but, more importantly, to 'lay your claim' to that portion of your work, doing away with the risk that other researchers working on the same topic as you and developing ideas similar to yours may undermine your claim to originality by going public with their conclusions before you have had the chance to complete your PhD thesis.[61] To the extent that, by investing some extra effort, you can avoid or, at least, minimize that risk, the time spent repackaging your work will be time well-spent. A *third*, crucial reason why publishing as you go can be a good idea (but which applies to published articles more so than to conference papers) is because it can help make your life much easier during your *viva*. No examiner will ever seriously consider failing a candidate who has published some of her work before defending her thesis. Your School's regulations are likely to explicitly contemplate as proof of academic quality the examiners' assessment that your work is 'publishable'. What better proof of your work's publication potential and, by extension, of its quality than the very fact of its publication? Publication is, therefore, proof of quality and, especially if your work is published in a respected journal, there is a presumption that, no matter what the views expressed in it are and no matter how much these may differ from those of your examiners, your manuscript meets the standard required to enable you to survive your *viva*. If your examiners can rebut that presumption, let them be your guests.

Two words of caution here, followed by a reminder. A first word of caution is that you should not attempt to publish your *entire* PhD thesis, even if broken down in parts, prior to your *viva*. Your work has to be original at the time of its submission and your School's rules may not allow you to enter work that is already in the public domain prior to the completion and award of your degree. Moreover, it is possible that your School has a policy specifically in the matter of publications, imposing upon candidates restrictions in terms of what they can publish (and where) while they are still registered as research students. Unless your School's rules impose a total ban on publications (which is unlikely), remember to save for your examiners the most interesting part of your work, i.e. the part of it that your PhD will not stand without, even if all the rest of your work were to have been published externally (it is only fair that you should do so, if your *viva* is not to be a sham). The next word of caution is this: do not assume that you can take 3 or 4 articles that you have produced previously, tie them together, for better or worse, and present them as a PhD thesis. Your School's rules will no doubt prohibit such a ploy and, once discovered, you stand the risk of (very) serious embarrassment.

And, finally, for the reminder: it is only *desirable* that you publish, *not necessary* as such. A good piece of work will withstand even the most rigorous examination and give you the result you are after even if you, your supervisors and examiners are the only people to have ever set eyes on it in the run up to your *viva*. Besides, 'published' PhD candidates remain, by far, the exception: nobody will ever look down at you for not having published some of your work prior to your *viva*. Having said that, do not shy away from attempting to publish as you go, fearing that doing so will be too time-consuming or that it might expose you to the risk of compromising your academic reputation in the event that several months or years down the line you should decide that you have 'radically' changed your mind about views you went public with at the time of your research studies (the author has more than once heard that argument brandished against publications in the course of one's PhD studies, and he considers it fallacious). If your work is neatly compartmentalised, loss of time will be minimal; and unless your work is genuinely weak, you are unlikely to change your mind so fundamentally that you would stand any serious risk of incurring the sort of academic blemish advanced, by some, as an argument against publications at the time of a candidate's research studies. Remember, examiners cannot fail to be impressed by a 'published' PhD candidate and they will think several times before they fail her or, even, require (substantial) corrections to her work. And, in the almost feudal, holy inquisition-type of setting in which your *viva* will be taking place, their decision is, at the end of the day, all that counts. If you can influence that decision in your favour through *legitimate* means (publications being, alongside a good manuscript, the only legitimate means available) then so much the better.

One final point: if you *do* decide to publish, remember to acknowledge your supervisors' help in a footnote and to clearly state that this is work you have conducted while preparing your PhD thesis. There are two reasons why you will need to do so. One is out of courtesy or, indeed, out of a debt of gratitude to your supervisors. It is your moral obligation to acknowledge their help and trust in you and the chance they have given you to fulfil your doctoral ambition. An acknowledgement is the very least that they deserve.[62] The second is one of a more practical order: you do not want anybody suggesting that your PhD is a compilation of work which you took up and completed *prior* to your registration as a research student. This is *not* allowed and doing it (or deemed to have done it because you have failed to take the necessary precautions) will no doubt land you in trouble. It helps in steering clear of such an obstacle to explicitly state that your published work is work that you have undertaken as a PhD student.

In sum, to publish some of your work as you go is something that you should consider, taking into account your own interests in this matter and making the best of your School's rules. Judiciously managed, external publications can be a helpful tool that you would be well advised to use if you are to come closer to achieving your end-objective: completing your PhD thesis in less than 3 years.

PART IV
YOUR *VIVA* AND BEYOND

15. Choice of examiners

There is not very much to be said here that has not already been touched upon, in one way or another, earlier in this short book. If you have done everything 'by the book', your examiners are unlikely to fail you, no matter how awkward or demanding they may be. At most, they will ask you to make some corrections which, however much detracting from the achievement of your objective to conclude your work as swiftly as possible, will not cancel it out either. Having said that, examiner selection *can* be of critical importance, considering the absence of very many procedural constraints on examiners and the impact of their propriety, their fairness vis-à-vis the candidate and her work, and their doctoral degree examination experience on the final result.

Some of the author's recommendations in connection with your choice of supervisors also apply to your choice of examiners. Whenever possible, try to designate as your examiners academics with an established reputation and with, at least, a modest capital of examination experience, rather than younger, over-ambitious academics who are anxious to make their mark at your detriment (for instance, by trying to impress their more senior and, usually, more relaxed fellow-examiners with their academically high standards or with their narrow focus on methodology). Academics with a publications' record in your research area (even if they are not subject experts, as such) are, no doubt, the best choice.

Your selection criteria should concentrate on your prospective examiners' (i) academic credentials and subject-matter expertise, as gauged by their publications record (even if their expertise is not on your specific research topic), (ii) their experience as doctoral thesis examiners (to the extent that you have sufficient information on the basis of which to assess their exposure to PhD thesis examinations) iii) their independence from outside interests (assuming that there is any material available to enable you to draw conclusions on whether or not they fulfil this particular criterion) and iv) the overall consistency between their ideas and some, at least, of the ideas that you are developing in your manuscript. This last point is crucial: to designate as your examiner an academic that you happen to fundamentally disagree with merely because he or she happen to be distinguished in their field and/or recognised area experts would be a singularly bad idea. As it is difficult to assess the academic 'flexibility' of your examiners and whether or not they are in a position to recognise good work when they see it (as they should), even if the conclusions reached in it or the methods applied to reach them differ from their own, you would be well advised to steer clear of academics harbouring views that are opposed to yours, unless you are familiar with their character and know them to be open to different ideas and not too narrow-minded in terms of their methodological concerns. It is for much the same reasons that area experts are best avoided as examiners, as they are likely to have strong views about your research topic which, if in conflict with yours, could land you in trouble during the defence of your thesis.

Another point linked to the one above is this: whenever possible, quoting in your manuscript some of the work of the academics that you expect to be appointed as your examiners is an idea worth considering. This is so even if you do not necessarily agree with all of the views they have expressed, from time to time, in their published work (provided, of course, that your points of disagreement do not touch upon fundamental issues). At the same time, although massaging your examiners' ego is acceptable, you will need to remind yourself of the importance of acting as an independent thinker. Merely paying lip service to your examiners' work is something that you will need to avoid if you are not to run the risk of coming through as an undignified candidate. Needless to say, you cannot afford to be seen to be pursuing your objective of earning your doctoral degree through *any* means, however unbecoming of an individual with scholarly aspirations and genuine academic pretensions.

What is worth remembering is that, at the end of the day, what your examiners are after is an intelligent piece of writing, testifying to the author's skill in synthesizing different ideas, elaborating on them over two hundred pages worth of text, drawing conclusions from comparing different pieces of information and making proposals or presenting one or two new ideas for future research. The limitations in space of your manuscript mean that there will not be endless room for you to discuss exhaustively every single one of its many facets. Writing a PhD is not, after all, about re-discovering America, as we have argued time and again in this short book. It is a manageable exercise that, with devotion, discipline and commitment, you should be able to follow through to its successful conclusion, satisfying any, including the most demanding, examiner.

16. Your *viva* and how to prepare for it

There are some good and some less good news here.

Starting with the less good news, there is something of a paradox about your *viva*: while this is likely to be amongst the most crucial examinations you will ever sit, there is relatively little you can do to *specifically* prepare for it. As it happens, most Schools do *not* organize mock *vivas* for the benefit of their students (although transfer events may, to some extent, simulate the conditions likely to prevail in your *viva*) nor do supervisors tend to encourage *viva*-related discussions with their students (more often than not shrugging their questions off or providing vaguely reassuring answers so as not to strike fear in candidates but, ultimately, because there is only that much they can do to prepare you for it). Moreover, doctoral thesis examinations are, in any event, characterised by vagueness in terms of what it is that examiners concretely look for in a candidate's work. Such is the generality in the specification of the *viva* examination criteria that, whilst some specifications are common to most institutions, these hardly amount to clear guidelines for the benefit of candidates or their examiners.[63]

The good news is that your *viva* is likely to also represent a challenge for your examiners (especially where your research topic is an original one or where your panel consists of relatively junior academics); that your examiners are not, *a priori*, bent on failing you, as long as you are capable of holding your own and are prepared to take a stand (and defend it, in a scholarly manner) both on specific aspects of your work and on some of the broader issues in your field of research (*viva* discussions ever so often tend to veer off in that direction); and that, if you have been consistent throughout the course of the period leading up to your *viva* and if both you *and* your supervisor are happy with your work, you are bound to be relatively well equipped for its defence, perhaps more than you can imagine. Without prejudice to the above, let us see what you *can* do to prepare for your *viva*.

As one can imagine, the most basic way of preparing for your *viva* is to read carefully through your doctoral thesis before you walk into the examination room (although you will also be taking a copy of it along to your *viva*, preferably one that is identical to your submitted thesis so that, if referred by your examiners to a specific page, you can find that page easily in your own copy). Remember, your doctoral thesis is your most potent weapon in this challenge and a good thesis is bound to do *some*, at least, of the talking necessary to get you through the one and a half hours that the average *viva* will last. Having said that, you *will* still need to defend your work, however well considered this may be and however confident you may feel about it, which is why you *will* need to thoroughly familiarise yourself with your work before your *viva*, avoiding the treacherous 'complacency trap' that a good thesis can lay for you.[64] The reason for that is obvious: it would be embarrassing, to say the least, and, possibly, suspicious,[65] for an otherwise good candidate to be confronted with questions to which he or she can provide no answer because he or she can no longer remember *where* in her thesis and *how* she has dealt with the point or points to which the examiners' questions relate. You will be surprised by how quickly you are likely to forget small but significant details of your work in the three, four or more months that may elapse between the submission of your thesis and your oral examination; do, therefore, read through your work carefully in preparation for your *viva* to avoid unnecessary embarrassment.[66]

Preparing for your *viva* should also involve reflecting on the questions that your panel members are likely to invite you to provide answers to. There are two types of questions you will need to address your mind to here. There is what one might call 'standard' questions and, then, there are questions that are somewhat more specific to *your* PhD thesis. Standard questions are bound to revolve around the idea of originality and how you think you have met it in your thesis (for instance, 'what is new about your work' and 'how does your work differ from that of your precursors?'). More specific questions are likely to concentrate on your work's main or purported strengths (for instance, 'what is the central finding of your doctoral thesis' or 'what ideas touched upon in your thesis could you further develop in future research and how?') and, more importantly, on its weaknesses. Your weaknesses or limitations you will have to acknowledge (some of these already in the text of your PhD thesis) and prepare for, ahead of your *viva*, remembering that, as an aspiring scholar, you will need to apply your critical faculties also to your *own* work, judging it in an objective, detached and professional manner. What that entails is your readiness to engage with and, eventually, to take on board sensible comments that your examiners might make and which you cannot avoid accommodating without showing yourself in a bad light, as a somewhat difficult candidate and an immature or inflexible scholar. If accommodating these comments means making corrections to your submitted thesis, as it often will, so be it. What is also worth keeping in mind here is that not all of your examiners' questions will be directly related to your research (if only because *you* are the expert in that particular field and challenging expert conclusions is no easy task even for a seasoned scholar): some of their questions will really be about *their* research. The sooner you realise that, the easier you will become immersed into what has the potential of developing into a more or less pleasant and, with any luck, stimulating discussion, that will enable you to enjoy what is, *a priori*, a demanding examination (but which, if handled with caution, need not be the nightmare some candidates may fear it might be).

Another way to prepare for the 'mother of all academic examinations' is one that has been touched upon earlier in this book: it is by choosing your examiners carefully (avoiding scholars who, while experts in the field, are fundamentally opposed to your approach, judging from their published research) and by familiarising yourself with your examiners' work before your *viva* (so that you can assess which angle they are coming from in their questions and work out what an appropriate answer to these questions might be). That you will need to quote their work in your doctoral thesis is something that has already been mentioned in this book, but which is worth repeating here (do not underestimate the importance of massaging, within logical boundaries, your examiners' ego; they are only human, after all).

On your handling of the actual *viva* there is little to be said that the average mind cannot gather through the application of common sense. Be civil, courteous and respectful (no matter how irritating your examiners may be; after all, probing is part of their job) but, also, firm if you are confident of the merits of your work (remember, your work speaks for you and you will need to do it the justice it deserves by defending it with conviction and to the best of your ability). Do not shy away from challenging, however deferentially, your examiners' views if you feel that there are solid, scholarly reasons for doing so (examiners *can* make mistakes and they are *not* immune to criticism). Accept warranted comments (but not too readily, so as to avoid unnecessary corrections to your thesis). Finally, remember to take time to reflect on and weigh carefully your answers (there is, at this stage, no particular hurry ...).

Finally, some advice is due on your presentation. While scholars are often associated in the public mind with rolled-up sleeves, thread-bear sweaters and dishevelled hair, there is *no* excuse for failing to appear well-groomed and suitably dressed for your *viva* (and not just because you are only an *aspiring* scholar who has yet to earn the dubious privilege of a disorderly appearance). Although a smart appearance will not *per se* salvage a poor candidate who desperately tries to defend a weak thesis, it can only add to the overall impact of your presence, suggesting that you are taking the occasion seriously (as you should), rewarding your supervisor and examiners with the respect that their hard-earned academic status and the solemnity of the event call for. Besides, it is not uncommon for an orderly appearance to be an indication of a methodical, well-organised mind, and that is precisely the impression you will want to convey to your examiners. You can revert to casual dress right after your *viva*, while celebrating the result! How long you will need to wait for the moment when there is a result that you can celebrate will mostly depend on you. Follow some of the advice dispensed through the pages of this short book and you may have to wait for that moment to come for less than 3 years.

17. Publishing your thesis in book form

Now that you are through investing the time and effort necessary to produce *and* defend a considered piece of research that your examiners have decided has sufficient academic merit to it to warrant the award of your doctoral degree you may want to consider publishing it in book form, as a monograph. If you are toying with the idea, which you may well be, for some of the same reasons as those highlighted in section 14 of this book, there are a few points for your consideration.

Depending on the subject and, most importantly, on the *structure* of your PhD thesis, publishing your work as a monograph may not be feasible, at least not without (very) significant reworking. Concerning the *subject* of your PhD thesis, suffice it to note that if this is so specific that the market for it would be limited, your chances of eliciting interest from a publisher would, perforce, be slim (publishers are unlikely to show interest in your work unless they consider it likely to be able to sell at least a few hundred copies of your proposed book). Concerning the *structure* of your thesis, you may care to note that while a PhD thesis may, at first sight, resemble a book (it is, after all, bound, it has a table of contents and an index and other trappings of a 'book') it is more of the exception than it is the rule for a doctoral thesis to be publishable as a book *without* the need for some adjustments. This is because the accepted format, language, type of argumentation, objectives and, ultimately, the audience of a PhD thesis differs, in many respects, from those that you would expect to come across in the case of a book. Exceptions *will* occur where a doctoral student – typically someone with publishing experience – has, from the outset, planned her work with its publication as a monograph in mind. The way that can be achieved is simple and it is one that has already been touched upon earlier in this book: it is by ensuring that her PhD chapters resemble book chapters, in the sense of being autonomous, self-contained pieces of work, which she *has* or *could have* published as journal articles (subject to less than dramatic changes) while still researching and writing her PhD. This, incidentally, is another reason why dividing your work, already at the planning stage, into manageable, self-contained parcels, makes good sense and is an investment worth making: not only will that approach enable you to finish your work sooner rather than later, without loosing your sense of direction along the way; it will also render its publication as a monograph considerably easier, narrowing down the investment in time and effort necessary for the conversion of your thesis into a book to the minimum required to update it with some fresh references and, possibly, to enrich it with material that you could not include in it for lack of space (remember, as a PhD candidate you are subject to a maximum word-count restriction, which should normally not apply to book authors, for whom *minima* rather than *maxima* are more frequent).

A doctoral thesis suitable for publication as a book without the need for a fundamental reworking should also be capable of being re-packaged as a series of journal articles. The author's advice to you is to take the monograph option and to only publish (some) of your work in the form of an article as you go along, as already proposed in section 14. This combination will enable you to derive the maximum benefit out of your work in terms of publications, both *during* and *after* your work has been completed, while, at the same time, ensuring a smoother ride during your *viva* (as we have argued earlier, a published candidate cannot very easily be failed by her examiners) and a modest source of income (and fame) from the sales of your book, thereafter.

If you do decide that publication in book form is appropriate for you and your work, the next stage will be for you to prepare a book proposal. It is important to think of your book as a separate entity from your PhD thesis and to plan a structure aiming at a coherent narrative flow. You may, for example, need to add new chapters or to omit some of the chapters of your PhD thesis. A good book proposal can be anywhere between 4 and 15 pages in length. It must include: a) a general rationale for the book, b) a statement on the expected audience/market, c) a brief review of the existing literature (particularly, any competing titles) and the place of the book within it, d) an expanded list of contents including an abstract for each proposed chapter, e) a brief *curriculum vitae* and f) one or more sample chapters for external review. You may choose to take the chapters you feel will need the least amount of revision from your thesis, but it is often more effective to send a revised chapter. The first chapter is ideal, but it may also be the most difficult to turn around for publication, in which case you may want to try re-working one of the middle chapters instead. Before the proposal is sent for review, you must attract the attention of the commissioning editor and possibly others at the publishing house of your choice. If one publisher turns you down, remember to try with at least one more before you give up on the idea (or rework your proposal).

What is worth remembering is that, if there *is* publication potential in your work (because of its subject and because you have planned and drafted your doctoral thesis in a way such that it can be published *without* considerable additional effort) you will need to try to have it published as soon as possible after you are through defending your thesis. This is so for two reasons, no less. One is that you are likely to still be in a 'writing mood' and to have the drive necessary to get you through this process; the other is that, the longer you wait before you publish your work, the greater the likelihood that this will loose some of its relevance and value, especially if its subject matter is topical and your research was of a so-called 'moving target' nature. You will need to be quick if you are to exploit a rare opportunity to ensure that the whole world takes notice of you and of your hard work. This is an opportunity worth taking, whether or not you have academic ambitions (for any aspiring academic, a book can no doubt be a passport to an academic career). And, remember, *scripta manent*: if published, your work will not collect dust at your School's library. It will, instead, be available for consultation by anyone interested in its subject area, for posterity, in the world's libraries!

Finishing your thesis sooner rather than later will bring closer the moment of the publication of your PhD thesis. While publishing one's PhD thesis in book format is not the main reason why one may want to take up a research degree in the first place, the prospect of becoming a published author after successfully completing one's work is strong enough an incentive for a candidate to strive to achieve the objective advertised in the title of this short book: finish their PhD thesis in less than 3 years.

18. Postlude

Writing a doctoral thesis requires no specific frame of mind. You do not need to be a natural born academic (although an inclination towards the discipline associated with scholarship will definitely help); nor do you need to be a natural born author (although a good command of the language and good writing skills are a must). A healthy measure of inquisitiveness and curiosity and a sharp critical faculty are, nevertheless, *sine qua non* conditions for your success in this endeavour, which is bound to test your mettle. Even more importantly, however, you will need to be disciplined, focused and committed to see yourself through the challenge of PhD-writing.

Your PhD has to be constantly present in your mind as something that you will need to deal with on a daily basis with *three* objectives in mind: one is the short term objective of continuously expanding on and improving your manuscript; the second is your medium term objective of meeting your immediate completion goals, as identified in your research proposal; the third is the longer term goal of finishing your PhD as soon and as well as possible. At the same time, while PhD-writing is not a part-time occupation, it does not have to (nor should it) monopolize your existence. But if you would rather do a thousand other things first, including week-long skiing holidays in Switzerland, wine-tasting trips to Hungary or month-long language courses in Sweden, it could be that this is not something for you, not necessarily because you lack the intellectual potential for it but because your priorities are different and, maybe, rightly so (*you* are the judge of your own happiness). At the same time, what is important to always keep in mind is that postgraduate research cannot and should not be an end in itself: it should rather be a temporary stop on your way to something more permanent and worthwhile, whatever that may be, which is why prolonging unnecessarily the experience of PhD-writing serves no legitimate purpose.

You will be on your own, most of the time, and you will need to discipline yourself. Neither your supervisors nor your School will do that for you, try as they may, through research seminars, regular meetings with your supervisors or other monitoring mechanisms. Nor are there any magical recipes for success: your work is the currency that will buy your way into success in this endeavour. Hard work and commitment can take you a (very) long way in a relatively short period of time; ingenuity, inquisitiveness and imagination will take care of the rest. At the same time, avoid taking any of the 'soul-searching rhetoric' surrounding PhD-writing at face value: you do not have to re-invent yourself to write a PhD thesis. This is something that any ordinary, self-disciplined, reasonably intelligent and naturally inquisitive person should be able to do. Be systematic and stay focused, follow your routine, take this project seriously, acknowledging what is truly at stake here for you (your sanity and self-esteem, no less), and you *will* prevail. Follow some of my advice in this short book and you should be able to attain your objective in less than 3 years.

Trust me: I am speaking out of personal experience.

ENDNOTES

1. There is at least one fundamental difference between a PhD in humanities and its equivalent in the fields of science or engineering, at least in the Anglo-Saxon world. Humanities and social science PhDs are about collecting data to facilitate original thinking, with the research topic being of the candidate's choice. Science and engineering PhDs tend to be about a tenured academic getting work done on an ongoing project, some times in teams, with the research topic being, often, advertised along with the studentship. PhDs in the US tend to differ from their equivalents in the UK in being far more course-work oriented, with the length of the actual thesis (or dissertation, as it is known across the Atlantic) being considerably shorter than the one required in the UK.

2. The mass proportions that higher education has progressively assumed in the course of the last two decades means that Universities have to 'cut corners' in terms of the assessment of their students and to formalize the way in which these are examined, allowing room for smart candidates to discover the keys to obtaining good examination results that may not always reflect their skills, academic acumen and future potential.

3. This antagonism is easy to explain: a PhD candidate is, effectively, asking her supervisors and examiners to recognize her, on the basis of her work, as their equal.

It is only natural that examiners, in particular, should view such advances with some reservations and that they should apply strict standards to decide whether or not to recognize candidates the privilege of the promotion to the status of a PhD holder.

4. This has not always been the case. Distinguished academics in previous decades did not always hold PhDs (or DPhils, as PhDs are, in some Universities, called). This practice has nevertheless changed in recent years, with the number of professional (tenured) academics holding PhDs having risen dramatically across the board (in some disciplines more so than in others).

5. Whether there is any justice in this criticism the author has not been able to decide. It certainly sounds counter-intuitive that written proof of one's analytical skills, drafting capabilities, motivation and stamina should disqualify their bearer for white-collar positions requiring, by definition, exactly such skills and qualities. However that may be, there is evidence that, at least in the Anglo-Saxon world, PhD holders are sometimes viewed with suspicion.

6. It is hardly surprising that some employers (admittedly, not the majority) are prepared to undertake some of the costs involved in the process of studying for the award of a doctoral degree, appreciating the added value of an additional PhD holder or two within their organisation.

7. Formal writing, in particular, is in the very nature of white-collar work, meaning that the practice that one will acquire while writing one's doctoral thesis will

stand one in good stead whatever profession one may chose to pursue later in life.

8.   As you are likely to discover, future difficulties, especially professional ones, will, in relative terms, fade into insignificance compared to those you were faced with during your research studies!

9.   George Herbert Leigh Mallory, one of the English mountaineers who took part in the first British expeditions to Mount Everest in the early 1920s, is said to have replied to the question 'Why do you want to climb Mt. Everest?' with the retort: 'Because it is there'. The frame of mind necessary to see you through a postgraduate research degree should, in some respects, be similar to the one that these words hint at, somewhat less heroic, perhaps, but, no less pragmatic and matter-of-factly.

10.   The author, for one, would have a good deal of sympathy for your predicament, should you harbour feelings similar to those described above. The author had some 6 years of professional experience under his belt prior to starting his PhD, three of which in private practice and another three as a member of staff of a respected supranational organization. Reverting to the status of a student was no easy task.

11.   However important your research work may be, your professional occupations should always be your priority if you decide you want to continue working while writing your PhD. Falling behind with your professional career or forsaking promotion opportunities because of a decline in your performance would be too high a price to pay in order for you to be awarded your PhD title.

12. The author remembers a final year research student having asked him, when he first registered for his PhD degree, whether he thought he would manage to complete his thesis before the 'big bang' in his field of research. This question haunted the author throughout the course of his research, motivating him to pursue his work doggedly and to avoid unnecessary delays.

13. There are more people pursuing postgraduate research degrees than there have been at any time in the past. To the extent that there is any truth to the old adage that 'great minds think alike', the probability of two or more people simultaneously working on the same topic and developing much the same ideas can no longer be deemed to be negligible.

14. This is something you will want to avoid, both because it could render harder your struggle with originality (see section 8 of this book), meaning additional work and delaying the completion of your work, but, also, because it could compromise or, even, altogether cancel-out the likelihood that you will be able to publish your work once you have completed it.

15. After having decided on the general field of his research, it took the author several months of active search to decide on his specific topic (including the time required to test his thoughts).

16. Somebody else's topic is unlikely to interest and motivate you as much as one which is well and truly your brainchild.

17. An unfortunate choice of research topic comes with no guarantee that you will, eventually, be successful at

narrowing-down the scope of your research in time for the successful completion of your PhD thesis.

18. The author knows of at least one successful candidate who changed topic altogether a year into her research and, nevertheless, managed to complete her PhD thesis successfully. Such cases are, clearly, exceptional and should not be relied on as sources of inspiration except by the most fool-hardy of candidates.

19. If you can reduce the subject matter of your research topic into a single sentence (however long) chances are you are on to something good.

20. This is why it can be advisable to only take up PhD studies after you have gathered a few years of professional experience (but not too many: maturity is, ever so often, accompanied by complacency, altogether incompatible with the conduct of research): more mature candidates are likely to have a clearer idea of their research objectives compared to candidates taking up their PhD studies straight after the conclusion of their first graduate degree, with little exposure to the 'real' world.

21. The author chose to write his doctoral thesis on a topic that he was by no means an expert on (far from it) but which was not, when broken down to its individual components, 'Greek to him' either.

22. Inter-disciplinary research topics, very much en vogue in recent years, also carry the risk of drawing candidates in discussions that they are not necessarily conversant with. If, for instance, you happen to be a lawyer by education, to veer-off in the field of finance or economics is to put yourself in a precarious situation.

23. On the issue of originality, see section 8 of this book.

24. On the issue of publications, see section 14 of this book.

25. The author is aware of the somewhat spiteful but not entirely unjustified derision with which one PhD holder is routinely treating another, no less bright and scientifically adequate PhD holder, for having written his thesis on an obscure, unimportant-sounding and marginal topic.

26. A polemical research topic is one that is so controversial that it is best avoided, not least because you cannot predict which side of the argument your supervisors or examiners will side with.

27. The author chose to write about a financial services sub-sector that was in the news constantly but which, surprisingly enough, was not regulated, allowing room for thoughts and proposals to be formulated on how its regulation might best be achieved.

28. It is important to distinguish here between a 'research proposal' and a 'skeleton'. The former is a detailed account of the topic that you propose inquiring into and of the sequence of steps that you would propose taking to reach your conclusions, while the latter is no more than a broad outline of the structure of your proposed thesis. Both are useful and it is only by producing a skeleton that you can then reflect on and elaborate on its individual details so as to produce a fully-fledged research proposal.

29. Do not underestimate the utility of devising at least a working title, however long this may be and however

much you are likely to revisit it as you go along. Your title should not be divorced from the contents of your doctoral thesis and should convey to the reader the underlying idea and objectives of your research.

30. It is at the end of the exercise that you will discover how valuable your planning was and how the time you spent producing your road-map was time extremely well spent. Comparing the original skeleton (jotted in red ink on two A4 paper sheets) to the final product of his research, the author discovered that the differences were fewer than one may have expected. This is because his skeleton (and, thereafter, his research proposal) was well considered and logically arranged, making it easier for it to stand the test of time.

31. It goes without saying that, compared to a piece of scientific research work, writing this book represented an easier task, with the author drawing almost exclusively on his own experience without having to look further afield in search of arguments to support his ideas. The underlying logic is, nevertheless, the same!

32. You do not want to give up too readily on a good research topic, since inspiration for another one is unlikely to come before long!

33. The author remembers that one of the contributors to the research seminars that he attended used to prudently caution students against digressing from their research topic merely because 'the world is connected to one's research'. It is not because abortion is linked to human nature that a legal analysis of its parameters conducted by a trained lawyer has to be converted into a study into

philosophy or human psychology (for which lawyers are unprepared, as a matter of education).

34. Aspects of your research topic worth excluding are, in particular, those that you are not at all conversant with, by training or experience.

35. The term is used here in its dictionary meaning, defined as a proposition that is supported by one or more arguments.

36. The uncertainty surrounding the definition of 'originality' is, to some extent, punctuated by the absence of research on the nature of doctoral studies or on the purpose of doctoral degrees.

37. If anything, the mere thought that you have something extraordinary to say should put you on inquiry, in case your enthusiasm has got the better of you, blinding you to more or less obvious weaknesses in your reasoning.

38. A self-doubting candidate is likelier to be able to produce a better, more thoroughly considered piece of work compared to an over-confident one who thinks she has thought of something genuinely ground-breaking only to discover, some time down the line, that her thoughts cannot withstand serious criticism.

39. To merely regurgitate what is already floating in the public domain will clearly not suffice. However, as Frank J. Dobie has aptly observed, an average PhD is about moving bones from one graveyard to another. While the author of this book would never want to encourage you to write nothing more than an 'average' PhD thesis (however much this may be better than no PhD thesis at all) what he believes to be equally true is

that all PhDs, including the most brilliant ones, involve a good deal of 'bone-moving' (even if less so than the less good examples).

40. Methodology is clearly far more important in the field of positive sciences, both for research workers and for their readers, providing evidence that all conceivable variables were taken into account and that the results arrived at are reasonably accurate, while at the same time helping readers judge the merits of what they read and recreate the process used to conduct that particular type of research.

41. A friendly relationship may, in the beginning, appear attractive, helping you approach your work in a more relaxed manner. Yet, it is unlikely to withstand the demands of a robust, critical assessment of your work as you make progress with it, which is why it is best avoided.

42. While it should be possible for you to change supervisor(s) if your relationship is, for whatever reason, less than harmonious (or if your research were to take a radical change of direction) this is something that you will want to avoid as it will inevitably entail delays and administrative complications, capable of detracting from your research objectives and derailing your planning for the completion of your work.

43. The author had to travel by airplane for over one hour and show his passport before he could meet his supervisor and attend research methodology seminars. That was still reasonable and worked out well.

44. This is, possibly, the only reason why writing a PhD immediately after your Masters' degree need not be too

bad an idea, as you are likely to have easier access to academic references at that particular stage than later on.

45. The author is grateful to one Professor from Queen Mary College and to one more from King's College, London for their readiness, several years after the author's completion of his Masters' degree, to furnish him with reference letters, without which the author would have been unable to take up his research degree.

46. In this regard, see our discussion on originality, in section 8 of this book.

47. The author is living proof that combining full time work with research studies is perfectly feasible, provided that your subject area is not entirely divorced from your professional pursuits, a bad idea in the first place.

48. The author boasts a reasonably good memory; however, with few exceptions, none of the surrounding text could jog his memory into reproducing the state of mind he was in when he left this or that blank so as to elaborate, later on, on his syllogism.

49. The author did much of his proof-reading on the way to and from work, while in public transport.

50. The first year will be your first experience of the intensive and solitary nature of graduate research study. Especially if you are coming directly from an undergraduate course, it will represent a dramatic change in the character of your hitherto academic experiences.

51. The reference is to the upgrade of your registration status from MPhil to PhD, for the purposes of which

you will need to persuade your department that i) you have accomplished substantial progress towards completion, ii) you have a clear sense of direction as to where you want your research to take you and iii) your doctoral thesis will satisfy the originality requirement for the award of a PhD degree. For the purposes of your transfer event you will typically have to submit a substantial piece of written work (two draft chapters or one third of your work), accompanied by a realistic, step-by-step account of your timetable for the completion of your research.

52. There is no way to summarize a huge piece of work unless you repeat it and this is something that you will want to avoid at all costs.

53. On publishing, see sections 14 and 17 of this book.

54. This should also allow you to think about the next day's work while you are asleep and, hopefully, to resolve open issues or to see things more clearly!

55. We will revert to this aspect in our discussion, later in this book, of your choice of and relationship with your supervisor.

56. Plagiarism strictly speaking refers to the *verbatim* use of another's language, not to the reproduction of their thoughts or ideas.

57. In academic circles, plagiarism is considered to be an act of dishonesty or downright fraud, with offenders being subject to censure up to (and including) expulsion.

58. Typically, a PhD thesis will consist of six Chapters, including an introduction and a chapter with the

candidate's conclusions on the research questions analysed in her work.

59. The quality of your work need not be the sole explanation for a rejection, which is why such an eventuality, however unpleasant, also needs to be put into perspective.

60. It is through your publications rather than your PhD that your work will become known to the outside world (unless your PhD is also published, which is not always the case). Few are those who will ever consult your PhD and, in any event, fewer compared to those who will read an external publication.

61. In this regard, also see our discussion in section 4 of this book.

62. The author regrettably forgot to do so and was, understandably, embarrassed. You may want to learn from his mistake.

63. 'Original' and 'substantial' contributions are almost universally required but what exactly it takes for a contribution to meet these criteria is not that clear. Other requirements common to the vast majority of institutions are that the candidate's thesis be located in the appropriate field and that it be the candidate's own work.

64. A *viva* can only safely be approached as a formality if you have published some of your work beforehand. No sensible examiner will ever fail a 'published' candidate, no matter how they may disagree with her views.

65. One of the less obvious but, nevertheless, very real objectives of the viva is for your examiners to ascertain

that you are the author of the doctoral thesis under consideration. If you have difficulties responding to questions of relevance to your doctoral thesis your examiners may assume that it is because you are not the author of 'your' PhD thesis.

66. The positive aspect of these three or four months is that they give you time both to prepare for your *viva* and to recover from the effort involved in submitting your thesis. You may want to use some of that time to relax, only reverting to your PhD thesis when you start preparing for your *viva*, looking at your work with a fresh pair of eyes and an open mind.